Not Held Down

FELICITY GRAHAM

Copyright © 2020 Felicity Graham

All rights reserved. No part of this publication may be reproduced, distributed, or transmitted in any form or by any means, including photocopying, recording, or other electronic or mechanical methods, without the prior written permission of the publisher, except in the case of brief quotations embodied in critical reviews and certain other noncommercial uses permitted by copyright law.

 A catalogue record for this book is available from the National Library of Australia

Graham, Felicity (author)
Not Held Down
ISBN 978-1-922337-85-6 (paperback)
978-1-922337-51-1 (ebook)
Memoir

Typeset Font 11/16

Cover and book design by Green Hill Publishing

For all the foster kids who feel silenced and misunderstood.

> SOME NAMES, PLACES
> AND EVENTS HAVE
> BEEN CHANGED OR NOT
> MENTIONED DUE TO
> CONFIDENTIALITY.
> (BASED ON TRUE EVENTS.)

CONTENTS

Author's Note vii
Prologue viii
Part One — NEW BEGINNINGS. 1
Part Two — FINDING GOD. 19
Part Three — FOREVER FAMILY. 27
Part Four — TRIAL INTO TRIUMPH. 67
Epilogue 137
Acknowledgments 141

AUTHOR'S NOTE

I did not write *Not Held Down* to criticise or belittle my past foster families or Department of child Protection, but I saw what the system did to my family and my friends. I saw what it did to me. I knew that it was easier to follow the crowd and become the stereotype – to do drugs or to get into crime. Especially if that was all you had ever known. I decided that I didn't want anyone to feel the way that I had; to feel hurt, unwanted, unworthy and a failure. I said to myself 'I don't ever want anyone to experience this self-hate', and in the hope that my story might help others, I knew my voice needed to be heard. I had so many ups and downs during this time, and sometimes the ups lasted a long time, sometimes only a few weeks. I had my heart broken so many times and I wondered what the future would bring. God saved me, and I loved and thanked him for it.

Some people hurt me a lot, and I shared some of those things, not to paint them in a bad light but to show that sometimes our anger makes us do things we would not normally do. It's all about learning how to say sorry and I forgive you. I have forgiven everyone who hurt me, and I loved them and wanted the best for them.

I hoped *Not Held Down* would be able to shed some light on a situation that is often left unspoken. This book would be my biggest achievement, it was hard, but so fulfilling and I'm glad I wrote it. Even if it only helped one person, I knew it would worth it. Some people might not like it, but it was my story and if it helped the right people - then that would be all that mattered.

PROLOGUE

'Mummy, Mummy, what's happening?' I cried out in my little 7-year-old voice. I kissed my mum's tear-stained face as we bid our last goodbyes. My 7-year-old brain was trying to comprehend what was happening as I sat in the car holding my favourite Pooh Bear teddy whilst looking out the window. We were driving further and further away from a house with many happy and sad memories. We reached our new home and our new life, but little did I know what the future held for me. We stepped into the house, ready to meet our new parents and family. The only family I had by my side was my big sister.

'Hello' said my new foster mum who I had known for quite some time; 'I don't know if you remember me, but we used to come over and see you, and look after you. This is my husband,' she said introducing herself. Being quite shy, I replied 'hi', in a small mouse voice. I did remember them a little bit and I had always thought they were nice, so I felt a little bit better knowing that I was with someone I knew. Even if all I wanted was my Mum. While Department of Child Protection (DCP) talked to my new parents I decided to look around. From my place at the doorway I could see that the house was big. There was a big lounge room to my left, a staircase in front of me, and to my right there was a pool-table and a hallway that led to the kitchen.

After a couple of minutes, three people came down the staircase. The first person was a guy, and he was older. Then came their other foster kid, and finally their special needs daughter. I'm not sure how

I reacted or how I felt when I first saw her, but I grew to like her. After meeting some of the family, Foster carer's came back inside, and they took me and big sister upstairs. In front of us, at the top of the stairs, the toilet and bathroom were separate. It wasn't big or small, it was an average size, but probably bigger than the bathroom back home. We then turned right and there were two bedrooms; the one on the left was Wade's and the one on the right was big sister and my new room – it was big!

The bedroom had two beds; one with a pink bed cover and one with a purple cover. We got to choose our bed, and I chose the bed with the pink blanket which was closest to the sliding door that lead to a balcony, which had an amazing view, but it was a bit scary for me.

In our new room we had a sliding closet to hang our clothes in and had a TV which sat on top of another set of drawers for our clothes. Once we were settled-in, DCP left. I was still a bit scared and I missed my mum so much, and the only person I had left was big sister. She was who I looked up to.

They had two dogs. One was a big old dog named Napoleon, and the other was a small dog called Ellie. They also had a big cage full of birds that were loud but pretty.

Part One

NEW BEGINNINGS.

'Every end is a new beginning.'

- UNKNOWN

If I had known back then what I know now, my life would've been a whole lot different. I would've known what my future would hold, and maybe, just maybe I could've done life a bit differently.

I can't believe seven years ago I was put into foster care, I thought to myself, as I laid in bed my first night in emergency care. I had so many thoughts running through my mind and I was afraid they would make me go crazy. I was thinking about today's events. It had been a beautiful day but I wished it hadn't been. I wished it had been raining, I wished it had been cold and grey, so that it would suit what a bad week I had suffered.

I had just left my foster home of seven years, but our issues had been building up for a while It started with arguments and fights. Me screaming: 'you never trust me' to my foster mum (it was true), and my foster mum replying with 'you are a spoilt bitch.' To be fair, it was my fault. I wanted attention, I felt unheard and unloved, so I said and did things that I regret. Things like sneaking around behind their back and losing their trust. It got to the point where there was no repairing our relationship – I had stuffed up big time.

It all started a couple of years ago when my sister swore at my foster mum, they argued, and my sister left. She went to live with our other sister, her partner and our niece. So, it was just me alone; with my foster parents and their three kids. I didn't have anyone with me. My home life got hard and the arguments were way too regular. I found comfort at school, where I would stay as long as I could, because every time I went home I knew an argument was waiting to happen.

I was lucky to have support from my teachers, but my foster mum didn't like that because she worked at the school. I never did anything horrible, but I did break their trust a lot (I was sexually abused, something no kid should ever have to go through. And it made me get involved in things that only adults should be doing.) And because my foster parents were strict pastors, they weren't happy when they found out. But I could never tell them why I did what I did.

All of this led to today, I knew it was coming. I had even told my caseworker through DCP that it wasn't working. But my two favourite teachers intervened – they wanted the best for me and did not want me to move. So yesterday they sat us down to work through some of our issues, and a part of me was hoping my foster mum would change her mind and be the mum I needed. I had gone to bed and was told to say goodbye to everyone; just in case I did leave the next day.

I hugged and said 'goodbye' to their 26 year- old daughter, who had been my foster sister for 7 years, with my eyes watering and chin trembling, trying not let any tears drop. I went to bed letting my tears flow onto my pillow and I was soon asleep. I woke up this morning to another bright, beautiful, autumn day and my birthday was only a week away. I went to school, I got picked up early for a counselling appointment and knew that if my foster mum hadn't changed her mind, then I could be moving today. There was even a chance I may need to move to Adelaide, as there weren't many places in Port Lincoln.

At school, my class gave me a goodbye card and I left. After my session with my counsellor of three years, I went home to pack. My body shook and my palms were sweating as I walked through the door. There stood my foster mum with a scowl on her red face, and as if she were in a cartoon, I imagined her having steam coming out of her ears. I was shaking with fear, you never wanted to make her angry, just as you never wanted to make a bull angry.

'Get her out tonight, I don't want to see her again. I don't want her here another night. I am never fostering again.' she spat to my worker.

One by one the tears fell, *how did I mess up so badly for her to say this* I thought. I ran upstairs not wanting to let anyone see the hurt. I started packing everything, letting the tears fall and my eyes became swollen and red. Once done, I looked around my room and the balcony that I had had for so many years. I turned and walked down the stairs, I said goodbye to my foster dad and their grandkids and walked out with my caseworker.

'Sorry she said that to you, are you okay?' my worker asked, even though she knew I wasn't.

'I am fine, now you know that this is what I have had to live with,' and with that she drove to a place outside of the city that I had lived in and to a little town where I would stay until someone new would take me in. Even as I recall this moment, I am looking up at the ceiling with tears trickling down my face, remembering the pain. I wasn't always a quiet crier, but I had to learn. I was never listened to in that house, I was always told 'I don't have time for your drama,' so I just kept it to myself.

Eventually it got to be too much, and I self-harmed. But then I chose to reach out to people, and I begged to get a counselor so I could talk to someone. I thought my caseworker never listened or supported me either, so I felt so alone. I had only ever tried killing myself once and it was at a time when my foster parents were on holiday. Their daughter was entrusted to look after me. I felt like I couldn't take it anymore. I did my research and tried suffocating myself, I sent a suicide note to my favourite teachers and I was put into emergency care.

When my foster parents came home, they said 'you aren't depressed, you just want attention,' and it hurt to be told that. But now I am out of that house and I am waiting and waiting. I'm not sure what I am waiting for, maybe for happiness? Or answers? Or a family to love me and accept me as their own? I Know I am sad though, because that was the only family I knew. I didn't have much of a family, my mum isn't a mum; my sister left this foster family before I did, and she lost her way, becoming a hurtful person. I was used to it in a way, as we used to have many physical fights, and she hurt me in ways too hard to even write down. But once she left our foster home, she became worse, she was not at all nice and we didn't remain close. My dad had left when I was two, but he recently started contacting me while he was at work, so that his wife wouldn't know because she didn't want him to have anything to do with us.

Luckily the week got easier, and I still got to go to school and see my counsellor. Finally, my birthday came around. It was lonely, but my new emergency placement family tried making it as nice as possible by giving me gifts. My eldest sister came and took me out for lunch; while my other sister opted to go and see her boyfriend instead. It was sad that the sister whom I had lived with the longest had become more verbally abusive and manipulative. As weeks went on, I started losing hope that any family would want me. *I guess foster parents only want little ones, because society has labelled teens as too hard work. I guess I was one of these teens*, I thought.

My depression got the upper hand many times, so I would cut and bleed to release the inner pain. I tried killing myself many times. Every Thursday night we would go to netball and footy practice. There was a tyre-swing hanging above a branch nearby like a noose,

I would put my head through the hole, but never had the guts to go through with it. After a month in emergency care I heard about an Easter Camp that was being held at a beach and thought *hell why not? I've got nothing to lose.* So, after all the necessary approvals from DCP I went; but I had to inform the camp coordinator that I had bad mental health.

The first night was good, I knew a few people from youth group and school, so I hung out with them. When it came time for a beach walk at night I stayed in the dorms and talked with a lady I knew from church and shared with her some of the stuff that had been happening; and about my mental health. It was good talking to someone, and she was helpful most of times throughout the weekend when I reached out to her. Every night I saw people begin to give their life to Jesus. I had gone to church and youth group, but I wasn't a 'Christian'. If God was so good, where was he in my life? Why would he make me suffer?

By Saturday night my mental health had gotten worse and I couldn't handle the pain any longer. The lady I knew and who was also my group leader throughout camp took me outside and she showed me the stars. I looked up and thought to myself *it's so beautiful, how can something be beautiful and not have a maker.* She prayed for me and something happened, something I couldn't explain. I felt at peace as though someone was holding me, like a rush of cool wind was passing by which made me shiver, but how? The night was still, and I had goosebumps. I was shaking, rocking back and forth like a mum cradling her baby to sleep, as tears wet my face, falling and chasing each other down my cheek.

I knew I had to give my life to God – it was my only hope. That night I said yes. I went onto the beach and bowed my head, *God if you really are there, then please give me a family who will love me and hold me, who won't give up on me. I just want to be loved.* With that last prayer, I went inside and pushed the thought out of my head to have fun with my friends. We stayed up late playing games, laughing, talking and sitting by the campfire.

Sunday morning came, and we were awoken by a loud banging at 6 am! The coordinator had a pot and spoon to wake us up, so we could go outside and watch the sunrise. We got up quietly, wrapped in blankets and walked outside. We sat in front of a wooden cross which was erected by the beach, silently watching the sky. I was in awe, the sky was beautiful, it was pink, red, and purple, and I knew there had to be a God!

After an hour of quiet time on the beach, we went inside to get ready for the day. We played games, sung worship songs and did bible readings. Some parents came for dinner; I saw how happy and proud the parents were of their kids and I wanted that too. I isolated myself from the others as it was getting too much for me to handle, but a parent I knew saw me and we chatted. I hadn't seen him for a few years, we used to drive up to where he lived and have dinner with his family. I told him about what had been going on and he joked he would kick his son out so I could live with him. After a while we parted and said goodbye. I walked around for a bit until I was introduced to a young couple who were friends of my group leader. This couple clearly loved each other, and looked newly married, and they had a cute baby girl who was a couple of months old. We chatted until they thought it was time to leave. *They seem nice*, I thought after they left. I had told them I was living in a little town where they lived also, and they said I am welcome to come and visit their church. I told them 'thanks, I will think about it,' even though in my mind I was thinking that I probably won't take them up on their offer. But I couldn't say that to them.

Easter Camp came to an end and a new week began, I decided maybe I will visit their church.

The week went quick and I was told that I was moving, but I didn't know where. I said 'okay' and went back to the city I had lived in my whole life, stopped at the DCP office and put all my belongings into my worker's car. I said goodbye to my emergency foster care mum and hugged her. She said me 'I am like your aunt – you can always talk to me, you are strong and are like our family,' and as she said this the tears came. It was the nicest thing anyone had ever said to me. She left, and I hopped into the car, 'you are going to a group home, but we have to talk to the boss first,' my caseworker told me as we drove. I was silent, my hands were sweating, and I was beyond nervous.

We arrived at the office and waited to be called in. After a few minutes we were put in a meeting room and a nice lady talked to us, telling me a bit about the place and it's rules, and after a while the boss came in. I was surprised, it was a lady I knew (her daughter was best friends with my sister when we were young), and my sister and I would call her 'mini mum'. Seeing her calmed my nerves. After our meeting I went to the house, it was like a jail, it didn't seem homely at all. The worker was nice and helped me put my stuff in my new room, I had a big room and the biggest bathroom in the house. Once I settled in my caseworker left and I had to fill in more paperwork. I was the only kid in the house, so it was quiet. The weeks went on and I got to know the workers well. One worker would take me for a drive and buy a tub of ice-cream each shift, it was amazing, it was our tradition and something I looked forward to regularly.

By my second month there I was no longer the only kid. There was a new kid and he was someone I knew, we had gone to the same school in the past and had classes together, so we got along straight away. We talked about our old school, the teachers and other kids. Then another guy came along not long afterwards and I became the only girl in the house, but they never treated me unfairly. This new guy and I got along well, he flirted with me and I guess I flirted back. My worker and I had kept up the tradition of going out to get ice-cream, so when we had two workers on, one stayed with the boys while my worker and I went for our drive and ice-cream.

Living there got more dreadful and I started to really dislike like it; sometimes my teacher would literally push me to where I was to be picked up from because I did not want to go back. The boys and I tried to make it fun though, and we would pick on one worker and be shitheads at times. I guess living in a group home does that to you! She got annoyed with us quickly and would call the supervisor, but whenever he spoke to us about it we played innocent. We found fun in doing simple things, like finding weird carrots and being highly inappropriate – saying things like 'Brucy boy' or 'Franky' while making moaning sounds, or we would just throw the carrots at each other.

If we wanted to give the workers a real hard time though, we would leave the house after curfew and laugh at her. I remember this one day, I wasn't in a good headspace and got angry at a worker. I left after curfew and went to the park across the road where I laid looking at the stars thinking and talking to God. I rang a friend and it was a Tuesday, she told me something that I wish I never heard, that our best friend's mum had died. I couldn't feel anything, I was just numb and kept saying 'no, please tell me you are joking.' She wasn't, and I started swearing like crazy. This couldn't be happening! The day before, we were supposed to go to the gym, she rang me and said that she couldn't make it because something had come up. I should've known something was seriously going on, as there was a change in her voice. We hung up and I sat there trying to process what I was told, *no one deserves something like this*, I was thinking when heard the worker trying to get me to come inside. I yelled at her. After a while, I stood up and went inside and slept, my thoughts chasing each other like in a game of 'cat and mouse.'

The next morning, I had to have a meeting because my behavior was 'unacceptable. I don't have a lot of self-control and if I am around people who mess around and are rude, I will be the same, so I wasn't surprised that they wanted a meeting. They asked me why I was out of the house after curfew the night before, I told them the news and was told to go talk to the counsellor. I went to school, and my best friend messaged me saying she needed to tell me something. After school I went to the gym and waited for her.

Lucy had been my best friend for years, we met at netball and when I moved school we stayed friends. My foster mum didn't like her, she thought Lucy wasn't a good influence, so I would go behind her back to hang out with her. Lucy was tall, pretty, with red hair and she was always there for me, even after petty fights. Once we had a fight over a pen, there were slaps and hair pulling, the definition of a bitch fight, but we always made up and stayed friends.

After about five minutes I saw Lucy walk in, we walked to the locker area, I was silent. How do you comfort a friend who has lost someone so special? She told me what I was dreading to hear. I saw tears prick her eyes, so I wrapped my arms around and hugged her. Our other friend and I decided we wanted to buy something special for Lucy to show her we loved and are there for her. We went to the jewelers and bought a necklace that had 'we love you' on the front, and we had our names put on the back. We had made sure it wasn't a locket because we didn't know what may be written on the inside. A few weeks went by, Lucy and I went to the gym as we had boxing classes (one of my favourite classes). During the lesson Lucy's necklace opened and it had 'mum' written on the inside. She laughed, but I was mortified. I kept saying sorry and she said it was okay, but I felt bad.

Life went on and I still hated where I lived. I called it 'jail'. At school I got bullied. I had always been bullied, so it was nothing new. I was a very hurt kid and even though I was bullied and knew it sucked, I started bullying others. I was horrible, calling people all sorts of names, especially this one girl. We had always had fights and said hurtful things to each other, and we were even put on a behavior contract. I was so focused on my problems that I turned a blind eye on how I was treating others. I was always a kind-hearted person who forgave easily, but there was a side to me that was horrible, bitter and mean.

I was also diagnosed with depression. I kind of thought I had it, but it felt horrible to be diagnosed with it – knowing I had a mental illness. I still had my original counsellor, then I got another one and so I ended up with two. They were both lovely people and I trusted them. Then I had to talk to the therapist that diagnosed me with depression also, so I had three. I didn't think I was that bad!

The year went crazy slow, I had been in the group home for three months and still hated it. I continued going to church, my faith wasn't strong, but I prayed. I had good and bad days, occasionally self-harming and having thoughts of ending my life. Occasionally I would visit my emergency care foster family, and one time I stayed there I contacted the young couple I had met at camp and went to their church. They were so welcoming to me. I loved being greeted by them, they just seemed so loving and kind. Their daughter had grown so much bigger, she was wearing the cutest lime green dress and I got to hold her. Their church was small, they invited me over for lunch after church, which I said yes to.

I stayed at their house which wasn't far from where I was staying, and their house was small and pretty. We had risotto for dinner, and then put their daughter Baby B to bed. We sat down and had ice-cream and the husband, and I decided to do a science experiment which was fun. He seemed like a fun guy and a good dad, something I never had. After watching a movie we chatted, I didn't tell them everything that had happened to me, just the basics. I thought if I told them all my problems, they would not want to deal with me.

The wife was a nice lady, caring, compassionate and gentle, she hugged me as I spoke about my past and I had to fight back tears. I couldn't remember the last time I was hugged and held, 'is this what a mothers care feels like?' I thought. What was I missing out on? I thought of how I wish I had this love and care, but instead I was waiting for a home. how lucky other kids are to have parents who care and love them. When Baby B woke up, I played with her some more, she was such a cute and lucky kid to have parents like she did.

When I was living with my first foster family, I had learned to bottle a lot of things up. I knew they loved me and probably were trying to help, but I didn't always feel it. I didn't know how to talk about my feelings and emotions, or what was on my mind. I had to be either in a good headspace or really trust the person. When I'm in a bad mindset I act out, I don't know what I am feeling, and my thoughts are wild – I can't catch them to see what is wrong. So, I lash out, become rude, or say something in a joking way, but really I am not joking I just don't know how to explain how I'm feeling.

That day with the couple I met at Easter Camp was no different, I would make little jokes or snide comments, I wasn't rude or didn't lash out, but I noticed I couldn't control what I said. It had been a great day though. After dinner I went home, I was sad to leave, I felt like I belonged and had heard from others they were a nice couple and I was glad I met them. I went home that night empty, wishing I had parents who loved me, who would do fun experiments with me or hold me as I cried, but I was doubtful.

The next day I went back home to 'jail' as I liked to call it. I called it jail so much, those around me began calling it jail as well. After living in the group home for about three and a half months, I started going to this foster carer's house for respite. A week later I was told I would be moving in with her. I wasn't given a choice, they just wanted to get me out of the group home. The lady was nice and already had another foster kid who was 5, and I liked her house. The transition started and the Friday before the big move was Lucy's mum's funeral. It was a such a sad day; her mum had been an incredible person and I cried a lot. After the burial we drove back and on the drive my worker said to me 'you won't be joining her, will you?' I didn't think It was the right thing to say, but that was her way of making sure I was okay and wasn't planning on killing myself.

When the Sunday came my favourite worker dropped me off and said goodbye and that she would miss me. I cried, I was going to miss her too, we had so much fun together and had shared embarrassing stories. One story was when we were sitting at the table talking, she picked up a wrinkly mandarin, I laughed at her and told a joke. She thought I was thinking of something inappropriate, and told me that wasn't what she meant. I laughed harder and said: 'what do you think I think it means?' (I think you can guess where she was going). I told her 'we need to clean your mind.' I was going to miss her and her amazing pasta carbonara, but we promised we would still have an ice-cream date again soon.

I knew this was going to be a new fresh start and one that I needed. I settled in well and things went smoothly at first, but then a week went by and I still had mental health issues. I think deep down inside I was hoping they would disappear, but they didn't. Some days were harder than others. By week two my new foster mum and I started getting into arguments, but we still had great chats at night with a coffee, talking about good and bad things.

I went for a lot of walks and saw my sister and niece who I had lost contact with. My big sister who I had lived with for the longest had left our sisters' house and had moved in with a new foster family. She had gotten out of control, and she didn't want anything to do with us anymore, so my eldest sister and I grew close and she became a main support. I loved seeing my niece, she was only 5 at the time and was a little character. I wasn't doing well at school and I was struggling since Lucy had moved to the public high school, so I didn't have any friends.

Week three of my new home came around and the tension grew stronger, arguments were frequent in the house. I also got a new boyfriend, he was clingy and always wanting to hug me, which I didn't want. I have never been good at relationships. I mean, I can't even last in a family and the previous boys I've dated haven't been good people, so I was very wary about dating.

I was still in contact with the couple I had met at camp. I sometimes slept over and every time I talked to them and visited them, I let them in a little more. They didn't run away or think poorly of me, they listened, hugged me and were there for me. I was glad I had people I could trust, but I was still sad when I visited them, wishing I had parents like them. The couple's Baby B was growing so much. She smiled every time she saw me, and I became known as 'Aunty Flick.

Things started going downhill at my new home, we argued frequently, to the point where I would walk out of the house late at night crying, it felt like my first home all over again. Sometimes we still had good chats in between and would scare my boyfriend by telling him we had a trap door where we put people (no I am not psycho). On a Tuesday in September after school, I was feeling suicidal for no reason in particular, it was just one of those days where I wanted to feel loved. This time I thought about hanging myself. I researched to see which way would be best and be quick. I sent a goodbye note to someone I was close to and they called my foster mum. She told me she would take me to the hospital which I didn't want, so I put on a smile and said I was fine. I knew I was not okay but I had to pretend. I didn't do anything to hurt myself, instead I went to bed.

After school the next day, I got picked up by my caseworker and was told 'the adults and I have decided it's best that you move out tonight,' and I was beyond confused. 'Did I mess up another chance of having a family and home?'. I wasn't sure what I had done wrong. When I arrived home, I went into my room and all my stuff was already packed. I just picked up my stuff, said goodbye, and we drove to the same emergency care I had come from prior to this family. I was happy about that at least. Not only did I get to stay with a welcoming, nice family, but I also got to continue seeing the couple I met at Easter Camp.

I needed to leave my church and youth group as I would be living in another town 40 minutes away. I was sad about this, but I would still be able to see them, and I was going to a youth conference with them in October in Adelaide. A few days after my new move I settled in. They had moved outside of the little town onto a block of land with a beautiful house right on the beach that was great for morning walks and having some quiet time. I still didn't know why I had to move, no one had told me. I was used to being left in the unknown, but I still would've liked to know.

Luckily every Sunday I would see the couple I had met at Easter Camp and their little girl who was growing every time I saw her at church. After about a week I finally found out why I needed to move. My foster mother thought I deserved two parents and not just a single parent like her. I guess I understood, I knew she wanted the best for me, I messaged her as I did to all my foster parents and said 'thanks for having me, it means a lot. I learned so much and I just thank you for giving me a roof over my head. I believe everything happens for a reason.' I liked to say thank you to all the people I have lived with no matter how it ended, as I am grateful to them for taking me in. I broke up with my boyfriend, which I wasn't sad about. I guess I wasn't sad because families have always broken my heart and a boy can't do any more damage.

The youth conference was coming up and I knew it was going to be a great distraction. We had to drive eight hours to get to where the conference was being held. We left the night before and got to spend the night at the couple I had met at Easter Camp, I met his mum while I was there, she was a sweet lady and I could see how her son had turned into such a nice person. The next day I got everything ready and was given a jumper for the conference by the couple from Easter. I had breakfast, played with Baby B and then my youth leader arrived to pick me up. I got in the car with my youth group friends and they asked about who I had stayed with last night, I told them they were family friends and we talked more about them. The drive was fun, lots of laughs, singing and dancing and I was so pumped for the week ahead. We slept in tents; the girls together and the boys together. We went to two separate conferences during the day for the youth and a joint one at night with everybody, it was held in this massive church and lots of people came. I loved all the speakers; they all spoke to me and throughout the week I grew so close to God, to my youth group and leaders, who became like a second family to me.

Part Two

FINDING GOD.

'She who trusts in the Lord will never be disappointed.'

— ISAIAH 49:23

Over the past year I have learned a lot, grown a lot and been through a lot. I left a family I had lived with for 7 years who sometimes treated me like family. Their house was two-storey, with a pool. I went to a private school, went on holidays around Australia to places like Darwin, the Great Ocean Road and others. I had good memories which, I tried to focus on, but the bad memories kept coming in and drowning the good memories. I knew they still loved me, but not in the way I needed to be loved. They would not have had my sister and I for so many years if they didn't love us, I knew that, but in the end, it wasn't what my heart needed. I thank them for the good memories.

Before living there, no friends came for birthdays, our hair was full of lice and we wore dirty clothes; most people would not allow kids to live like this. Being in care had allowed me to make friends and have them come over, if only the system had always been that helpful. I remember one birthday I wrote my foster mum a card – 'happy bitch day', it was a mistake. I was only 8, I did love them, and I knew they wanted the best for me. They did things that they regretted and had done them out of anger. I was so angry with them back then, but this conference had helped me to see the bigger picture and even though they hurt me, and I hurt them, I still forgave them.

I was lucky, I realised I could have fancy stuff and nice clothes, but in the end all my heart wanted and needed was to be loved. To the world and the care system I was just another foster kid, another teen in care, but I just wanted a home and to be loved. I didn't think it was asking too much, it is one of the rights of a child, but the system is broken. It tried breaking me and it did. I didn't have my own faith at this time, even though I had been raised in a Christian home. I went to church regularly and as a young kid I would even call from my balcony 'happy birthday Jesus' on Christmas Eve, but that was it.

Easter Camp opened my heart. I wasn't listened to by anyone, the system that was meant to help me, ignored my pleas and I was lost. God was my only hope and I knew I had nothing to lose. I thought about all thought of these things one night at the conference, and I realised that being fostered and being in care was hard, no one wanted me, they thought I was too much to handle. I grew a lot throughout the conference. I began raising my hands during worship time, for the first time I prayed for someone and for the first time I spoke to around 300 kids and told them about my life and how I became a Christian.

One night while laying on my bed, I thought *if what I am feeling here at conference is real, then God is real, and he hears me* Would this God forgive me for being so mean to others? I have called people names, sworn at them and used foul language. Would he forgive me for the bad things I have done, like getting into stuff that was not meant for kids (only for adults), even though I thought it was the 'norm' as a kid? Would he forgive me for not trying hard enough when I was abused? Would he forgive me for not fighting to stay in a family, because obviously something was wrong with me as I couldn't last in families? I didn't know the answer to these questions.

The speakers at the conference helped a bit, but would it be the same for me? I wasn't sure, but I wanted the conference to last longer than it did. Unfortunately, all things must come to an end and we drove home when the conference had finished once again. The drive home was equally fun, but as we were nearing the place where I was currently living, reality hit me and I realised that I was going back to a life of the unknown. To a life of waiting for a family to want me, and I didn't want to go back. And with that thought, my lip trembled, and my eyes burned as I tried to hold back the tears, *I'm not ready to go back to my reality, can't I just start a new life?*

Soon enough my eyes hurt from holding back the tears, I couldn't hold them back anymore and I let them flow. It wasn't long until someone noticed me crying, I didn't want them to notice, I didn't want them to worry. I told them my concerns and they prayed for me, they prayed that I would find a family who will love me and who would be the parents I needed. They made me cry even more and I didn't know what I did to deserve such an amazing group of people who cared for me and saw me as family, but I thanked God for them.

Before I got dropped off, we went to the couple from Easter Camp's house to give back the jumper they had loaned me, and when I went inside, still sad from the drive and no doubt my eyes were still red from so much crying, the nice lady noticed. I told her why I was sad, and more tears came out. I was a mess but she didn't seem to care, instead she hugged me. A hug I wish a mother would give me and she stayed hugging me until I felt better. I don't think she knew how much that small act of kindness meant to me. I said goodbye, thanked her, said a quick hello to Baby B who never failed to make me smile and got in the car for another hard week.

After the conference the youth group were asked to write and share a little bit about the conference and what we learned. So, I pulled out my notes and wrote some stuff that stood out to me. I wrote about how before the conference I was lost and had learned God loves lost things. I wrote a bible verse that stood out for me and a heap of other things. Sunday came, and I was nervous, even though my church did not come close to the 300 people that I spoke to at the conference. When my time came to speak, I took my bible and my phone up to the pulpit, and because I had my bible all my youth friends start calling me pastor Flick.

Everyone started clapping and once they stopped, I started reading and talking about what I had learned and about the things God had taught me, 'I was lost but I learned God loves lost people.' Once I was done and church finished, I had people come up to me, people I knew well and people not so well, they commented on how well I spoke and how powerful it was. I was happy that I had such a supportive church who lived up to the name, because they were for sure a Family Church. During the week after the conference, I grew in my faith. I started praying more and tried to love God and forgive and trust him. It was hard to trust God, especially when two placements had broken down, I had moved four times that year and didn't know what would be happening in the future. Would I get the home and family I had always dreamed of and longed for? I had no idea. At the conference, I learned that trusting God isn't just for when things are going well and when the future is clear. Trusting God is when the future in front of you is foggy and you have no idea what tomorrow will bring, but know somehow it will be okay.

I grew so incredibly close to God the weeks after the conference, I gave him my broken heart. I had been angry at God and prayed when I wanted something in the past, but I didn't have a relationship with him until then. After the conference, life was as hard as it was before, but I knew I had to trust God. Before I had questioned if God was real because if he was real then why had he left me when I needed him. Where was the God I had learned about in Sunday school? During the conference I had felt this overwhelming sense of love and peace wash over me for the first time in my life. I felt the presence of God and it was like nothing I had ever felt, it was unexplainable from then on, I knew there was a God.

Even though I felt so down and horrible, I knew every time I opened my Bible that God was there holding me. I don't know how I went from hating God and thinking he isn't real to knowing how much he loves me, and I wouldn't change my faith for the world because with him by my side I didn't feel as alone. I am just so glad I have my friend Lucy, my youth group and my church that were there to pick me up when I fell. Who supported me and encouraged me, never left my side and prayed for me. Seeing their faith was what I needed, I wanted that trust, love and happiness. The week after speaking at church I prayed and listen to worship music to encourage myself. I tried trusting him and I prayed that he would give me a great family. I prayed he would bless me with a mum and dad who would love me, accept me and want me. Who would see me as someone worth fighting for, someone worth loving and investing in. I prayed that he would give me parents who saw past my flaws and saw hope and potential. I prayed that he would give a family who wouldn't hurt me and who wouldn't give up when I made mistakes, as I felt my own biological family had. I prayed so much and so hard. I would go down to the beach sit there and pray, pray until I had no words. I didn't know if he would answer my prayer, but I gave this whole relationship with God a go.

As the week drew on, I was called into DCP's office for a meeting, I knew no matter how nervous I was and how this meeting would end, I knew I had to trust God. It was all new for me, but I wanted to give my relationship with God my all. So, as I was sitting in the office watching my all-time favourite show 'the dinosaur train' I was rudely interrupted by my worker calling me into the room. I was a bit scared, worried I might have to move again or what would be happening now. All these questions were filling my mind and almost suffocating me, I felt it pulling me under. When they called me into the room, they introduced me to a lady and was told a couple who call me 'Flick' wanted to foster me. I knew few people called me Flick, but most called me Felicity. The adults who did call me Flick I thought would never foster me. 'Do you want us to tell you or to read the letter they wrote?' they asked. 'I will read the letter,' I replied eager to know who would want to foster someone like me. As I read the letter, I knew who it was straight away, fighting back the tears. I was happy that I was finally wanted, and I had my answer.

Part Three

FOREVER FAMILY.

'Family isn't DNA, its who brought you in, loved you for you and stood up to do what no one else did.'

I never would've thought it would be the couple from Easter Camp who would want to bring me in and call me their own. I had to fight back the tears that pricked my eyes. It was a beautifully written letter and I knew straight away what my answer would be. I was excited and nervous about the decision I had made, as I left the office and went back to the house, I couldn't wait to ring my new foster parents. My emergency care foster mum said I should answer the phone saying: 'hi dad.' I had a feeling that this might be the last time I would ever move, I just hoped that they would give me a chance and love me. After dinner, my new foster dad rang and I answered 'hi dad,' it felt strange saying that. I had never had a dad, could this my chance to know what it's like to have a dad? This was all new and one thing I learned in the past year was new things are so scary! We talked on the phone and I was asked when I wanted to move in, and I said 'as soon as possible.' I had waited so long for a place to call home. So, we decided that I would move the next day, which was Friday the 13th of October.

I told them that I planned to stay with a friend for a night, so I could speak in front of the church about the conference. I went to bed that night excited and thanked God for answering my prayers I just hoped this would work out, because I don't want to destroy such a great family and my relationship with them. Friday couldn't come any quicker and before I knew it their car drove into the driveway. I was so excited. They knocked on the door and hugged me.

I said goodbye and thank you to my emergency care family, who have been there for me whenever I left my placements. On the drive back to my new home I had a massive smile on my face. I didn't know what the future would bring, but I was happy they asked me to be their daughter. At home my new bedroom had a massive bed, it was a four-poster queen-sized bed and it was beautiful. On my bed was a teddy rabbit called Harry that they brought as a welcome home present, (Baby B had a white bunny). I had another teddy which was a sloth that I got when I first moved to the group home because my caseworker took me to Kmart to make my room mine. As I was buying stuff I saw a soft toy sloth on a random shelf I told my caseworker he was homeless like me and I want to keep him. And that sloth has held all my pain and tears, and now he has Harry as a friend!

I went away to my friends for the weekend. It was good to catch-up, but there were a few issues and I wish I had stayed home. The church was good though, so that was a good thing. By Sunday I couldn't wait to go home. I loved saying that... home. I had found a place I could call home, but I had to keep a wall up, I had to protect my heart. I've been hurt by other families as well as my own, so I couldn't let myself be that vulnerable - not yet. I have to let my heart take its time - I knew it would take time, but I didn't know how to voice that to them.

I am never good at voicing what's wrong and I guess that's what happens when you had to learn to keep everything bottled up. But I didn't have to worry about it yet. When I got picked up and we went home they wanted to post on social media to welcome me into the family. They measured me and everything, it kind of made me feel like I was important, and it made me feel happy. The post went something like this: 'On Friday we had the joy of welcoming our second daughter Felicity 'Flick' to the family. 157cm long with big bright eyes and lots of amazing curly hair. Welcome home sweetheart.' It felt good to be welcomed home.

School started again, and I arrived at school a bit happier, and I got to share the news of me finally having a new home and new family. I was sad that I wouldn't see my church or youth as much, but I knew this was a fresh start. My favourite part of everyday was coming home and playing with Baby B. Spending time with her always made my day and every night I got to read her a bedtime story. And if I just wanted a little bit more time with her then I would read her two. My foster mum went to bed early, so I didn't see her as much at night, I was used to late-nights as I always had them, so sometimes I would stay in my room or go and hang with my foster dad and we would have great chats. He was the dad I had always needed; he was always genuinely interested in what I had to say and listened to me. Sometimes I would talk a little about my life and the challenges I faced, opened-up just a little bit.

School was good sometimes, but when I was stressed and overwhelmed I messaged my foster mum. Messaging her made me feel reassured, that I had nothing to worry about and she would remind me that I was smart and that she was proud of me. It was good to have someone be proud of me, I had rarely had people be proud of me. I love having these new foster Carers as parents they were always there for me, and they were the parents I never had. When they hugged me, especially when my foster mum hugged me, I felt like I was home. It was a hug only a mum could give – a hug I had never experienced. So, when I came home from a bad day, just being held by them made me feel safe and it helped me feel like I belonged. I felt like I was home. Sometimes when they were doing something together with Baby B, I pictured myself stepping back and seeing what a perfect family they are, but it also made me worried. *They are so perfect; do I make their family better?* I hope they don't decide that they made the wrong choice. And just in case they give up I know I shouldn't get my hopes up too much because I know from experience that I was like a tornado. I destroyed everything in my path.

As my first week with them came to an end, I went to a youth event which is where my foster dad was going to present a speech. This youth event happened once a term, where all the youth groups came together. It is always a good night, and we got to reunite with people from the Easter Camp which was so much fun. A lot of people introduced themselves to me, and I hadn't realise how many people knew about me, my new foster parents liked to tell everyone. I never knew I was that special. I thought that maybe they would stop seeing the good in me in a few weeks, because why would they when barely anyone else did?

One lady introduced me to a girl who was a bit older than me, her name was Georgia; she was quiet but seemed nice. I went inside and sat with a close friend Maggie who I had been childhood friends with, I was sitting with her and her cousin. The youth event started with music. While we were singing, I would sometimes go to my foster mum and then back again after the songs. My foster dad introduced himself and mentioned his family when he said my name, I got embarrassed because everyone looked at me. We then played a few games, had food and chatted. After all that we went home, and I went straight to bed, I was so tired from all the interaction. I love talking and getting to know people but being around a lot of people gives me anxiety and I get stressed and hide away. The weekend went quick, with not much happening it was a relaxed weekend. I did a bit of homework but hanging with Baby B was more fun.

Another week of school went by, which I got to finish a day earlier because we were going on a road trip on Friday – it was time to pack. I was still a bit unsure and wary of how long this would last, and I was worried that my foster parents would see the bad person that I was. When the weekend came, we were ready for our trip, which was heaps of fun. I have always loved long drives because it's pretty seeing the different places. I am so grateful for my first foster carers for being the main reason for my love of car drives.

While driving we chatted, laughed and sang. We also stopped off at a few places and took selfies. We were on our way to a wedding, which was roughly 6 hours away but it was taking longer because we were stopping along the way. When we arrived, we hopped out of the car and were greeted by the couple who we were staying with. The people who we were staying with for the weekend had a dog, who had puppies and they were ADORABLE! So I spent most of the time playing with them, because who doesn't love playing with puppies?

I remember, growing up, I had a lot of animals; I had dogs and rabbits and birds and cats! My first ever pet (that I can remember) is a little black dog named Blacky. He had a bit of white on him when I was a kid, I had seen him in a cage at the pet shop. Looking back at it now, the cage he was in was way too small. He had licked my finger and that won me over, even now I'm easily convinced to do things! I went home and begged my mum to have him. The next day I got to take him home and I was so happy! I then got another dog a couple of years later and she was white, so me being 'little miss state-the-obvious', I called her Snowy. She became my best friend we did everything together. I would roll the ball to her and she would kick it back to me and she was a very smart puppy.

One day she got taken to the vet while I was at school, and when I came home I looked everywhere for her I was in tears until mum said she was at the vet. But when she never came back mum told me she was pregnant, so she got taken away. I was distraught. It seemed that whenever we got a pet it, would get taken away, it would die or run away, we only ever kept Blacky. But a few years later mum, got me another puppy and I called him Buddy. He was so small and he was cute, but crazy. I loved him so much. But I wanted another puppy after a few years with Buddy, so my sister and I bought another dog without anyone knowing and we called him Buster. I loved him, but Buddy didn't like him, so we had to get rid of him. My sister and I got in a lot of trouble, so I never did that again. I trained Buddy and would take him for walks whenever I visited mum as I grew older. I realised the environment that I grew up in was worse when I was a kid, which I didn't think was possible.

For some reason, mum never let my sister ever wash the dogs, and she rarely let us walk them or feed them because she claimed that she fed them (even though they were so skinny). Mum was never good at looking after living things, especially my sister and I. We were living in mess and eating food that had gone off, but it was all I knew. I am so grateful because even though the system had broken me, I am still glad that I was not neglected as badly as I had been when I was growing up. I don't talk to my mum much, which I am fine with and though it might sound harsh, being around my new foster parents make me feel more at home. I love my mum, but she hurt me so much. I know she was trying her best but that doesn't make the pain and what she put us through any less painful.

After playing with the puppies I went inside and hang out for a bit, while also setting up the couch that I was sleeping on. We had dinner and went to bed, but it was a bit hard to get to sleep and I woke up a during the night, so I was tired when I woke up in the morning. Getting ready for the wedding, I wore the dress my foster mum wore for her wedding reception. It was a white summer dress and I loved it; I also wore a flower crown. My foster mum took a photo of my foster dad and I in front of the mirror getting ready. It was a good photo, and I felt genuinely happy for the first time in a long time. The wedding was beautiful and after we had a family photo, I started to think that I have moved in with a family obsessed with taking photos!

We went back to the house, where I played with the puppies. My foster dad and I went for a walk, it was good having quality time with him, I never knew how much I needed a father. I had just learned to live with and move on from not having my dad in my life, it had never really affected me. I never had to think about it but spending time with my foster dad made me realise how much my heart desired to have a father.

After my foster dad and I came back from our adventure, where he taught me things and told me facts, I stayed home while my new foster parents and Baby B went to the wedding reception. While they were away, I played with the puppies, sat around and napped. After maybe two hours my Foster mum came back and went to bed with Baby B. I went back with my foster dad to the reception, it was awkward meeting people but after a while I felt comfortable. I met a chick called Felicity and we chatted, she was funny and nice. I then danced with a few people before my foster dad and I went outside, and he did a father-daughter dance with me – something no father figure had ever done with me. By the end of the night I was tired and ready to just crawl in bed and sleep for a week. We drove home and quietly went into the room and to bed trying not to wake my foster mum and Baby B.

On our last day there we all just hung out, and my foster mum and I were on a swing set talking. I was really happy that I had met someone so special and at that point, I knew it was going to hurt like hell if they decide they did not want me anymore.

We packed and got ready to go, and soon enough we were in the car ready for our journey back home. I got to sit in the front which was fun. The car drive was lots of fun we laughed, sang and joked around, and I knew that this right here was worth the wait and it would be worth the pain.

Once we got back from our little holiday, we got back into the swing of things, school and work, and just normal home life. Nothing significant ever happens at school. I get bullied and fail in my schoolwork and come home, play with Baby B and read her a book. Every day I dreaded school, and emailed my foster mum (sometimes my foster dad) and asked to be allowed to go home because I hated school so much! The week ended and the weekend came. On Sunday we had to pick up Georgia, the girl I met at the youth event. It was so awkward, and I had to give up my spot in the front seat because it was the nice thing to do, but I sucked it up and got to hang with Baby B in the back. I didn't know until later that apparently, I glared at Georgia the whole time. I guess I have a resting bitch face when I'm around new people. After church, Georgia came over for lunch and hung out, of course as the pastor's daughter my foster dad is always asking me to talk to anyone around my age, so I had to be nice.

In the car, on the way home, I taught Baby B praise Jesus (putting her arms up) and taught her how to clap. It was adorable, and she was so proud of herself. When we got home Georgia and I took Baby B for a walk to the park nearby. I got to know Georgia better, she seemed like a nice person and was easy to get along with. Baby B loved the swing and we had fun with her, it was kind of nice to be able to spend time with someone who was around my age.

My relationship with God was also fairly strong. I read a lot and it was good being in a Christian home as it helped with my walk with God. During the week I was reading the bible that was given to me earlier that year when I gave my life to Jesus, and there was a bible verse that stood out to me. It was Romans 8:18 'for I reckon that the present sufferings don't come compared to the joy that is to come' and I felt that God was wanting me to give it to Georgia. Yes, I have prayed for people and laid hands on people. But I haven't given a pretty stranger a bible verse.

Georgia, as far as I was aware, wasn't a Christian, so I just pushed it aside. But every day it was nagging in my mind and I decided to do it, but when Sunday came around, I didn't have the guts. After a while, I finally got up and went up to her, all shy and awkward and told her the bible verse. She seemed happy that I had said that to her, almost like she needed to hear it, and she thanked me. After that day we became close. We hang out so much and were good friends, and a part of me was glad I listened to God and I knew he was up there smiling knowing that everything that he had planned worked.

A lot happened in the first month of living with my new foster parents, I started trusting them a lot more, but I still had a wall up and was telling them they would for sure give up on me. I went on a small holiday with them, I gained a new close friend from just one bible verse, and for once in my life, I finally found a family who loves me for me (at least for now anyway). I also learned that my foster mum was an amazing cook but couldn't bake at all!

I loved everything about where I lived, and it scared me so much I went through every day scared that they would decide they had had enough of me.

My foster mum took me to a city in South Australia for the weekend where we went shopping, and we stayed at my foster dad's mum's house, who I met before I moved in. She was an amazing lady and I also met his sister. We went to the mall and my foster mum bought way too much stuff and wouldn't let me see the price tags, because I didn't want her buying me stuff. I didn't deserve it, I deserved bad things for the bad stuff I had done. My foster mum claimed that she had to make up for the 14 years of my life that she wasn't my mum for.

On the last day of our weekend I got to meet all the grandparents. I got to meet my foster mum's mum and stepdad, and they were nice. I even met my foster mum's heart-adopted parents Ardy and Lizzy, who were cool. Heart adoption is an awesome thing, that I later found out was something that runs in the family. My foster mum met this couple at church and the short story is she now calls them mum and dad and has a good relationship with them while also being close to her biological mum. I only ever got to experience a grandparent love once, but I don't know my extended family well.

I had so much stuff when I got back home, it felt good to be spoiled even though I didn't want them spending money on me. The flight home was nice and quick. I am not always one for flying I can get anxious but once in the air, it's really pretty and fun. I liked going away, it gave me a break from school, but it sucked coming back and having to go. I was happy when we got to see my foster dad because he didn't come with us on our trip, so I got to spend time with him and annoy him.

On the trip my foster mum got me a bracelet that said 'I got it from my mama', so from that day on I started calling her mama. That and also because I couldn't bring myself to call her mum, that name was like a bad vibe. I never had a good mum so I didn't like using the word "mum" as it was a good meaning to me and I felt like she deserved a better label then my biological mum so mama suited her. She was the first foster parent I ever called mama. She wasn't just a 'My Foster mum', she was special and the mum I never had. Before meeting Mama I didn't know what a real mum was now I do and we have the best mum daughter relationship, and My Foster mum went far and beyond to treat me like her own daughter.

It was the same with my foster dad, I couldn't call him dad because my dad wasn't around, and my foster dad wasn't like him, so I stuck with his first name and called my foster mum mama. I was blessed with the best, and every night I prayed and thanked God for answering my prayer and giving me more then what I had prayed for. Baby B started to be on the move more and pulled herself around. Sometimes, if my door was opened a little bit, she would crawl and push my door open when she saw me. She would have the biggest grin on her face and would laugh. She would go right into my room like she owned it, so I would play with her because homework didn't matter as much.

Ardy and Lizzy, who I met when I went away with my foster mum, came down for a few nights and it was good getting to know them. I was really happy that all the extended family saw me as their family and loved me as their own. I was worried that maybe they wouldn't accept me, but they were nothing but nice and caring. Never in my life had I met people who were genuine and were loving, this world doesn't deserve people like my new foster parents and their family. But I am so glad I found them, and I don't have to keep searching for a family.

Soon enough, we were getting ready for carols which my new foster parents were organising and running. Georgia and I helped as much as we could and looked after Baby B. Georgia and I became pretty close friends, we would hang out a lot and she saw us as family, and it was good to have a friend to laugh with and hang out with. When I get comfortable somewhere, I start saying things without thinking or in a joking way because I don't know how to voice my feelings and fears. It's something that I found hard because I never really had anyone I could talk to. I never talked about my problems and kept it all a secret.

So sometimes I would say things like 'you guys won't make it to Christmas, before then you will give up on me.' They would always reassure me but still, I was worried that they would give up because everyone else had. All I did was destroy families and relationships, and I hated it. But I tried to not worry about that, even though it was so hard. When carols came, we were all ready to go, my foster mum's mum had come over to help with Baby B who got sick that weekend. Big sister also came with her new boyfriend – I couldn't keep up! She moved a bit more than me; she was always running away and being out of control. She had left our sister's and they stopped talking because that's how toxic my family was.

Baby B got everyone sick: my foster mum's mum and my great-grandma were throwing up. My foster mum and I felt sick, but we didn't throw up and I spent the whole day laying on the cold ground trying to get better. I was just happy that I wasn't throwing up! After a few days of recovering, we got better.

I hadn't realise until that night how incredible my Mama's voice was, it was angelic, I was so jealous. Georgia and I were sitting on the ground and at one stage Baby B (who was sick) was so tired and sitting in my lap. She wouldn't let me leave her and I felt so bad for Baby B, I hated seeing my baby sister sick! But Georgia took the cutest photo of me holding her. By the end of carols, I was so ready for bed, I went on stage and congratulated everyone who sang and took photos with my new foster parents because, as I have said, they are one to take photos! When we got home, we had an after-party where Georgia and I pegged everyone and then went into my room to chill.

I never really bothered with presents, but my foster dad and Mama were important to me, so I wanted to get them something special. It had to be something that had meaning. I decided to get them a poster with four elephants that had our names on it with a letter which talked about family, and how it isn't about blood all the time but how you can choose your family. People always say how you can't choose family, but if you don't have one or it's toxic and bad like my own, then yes indeed you can.

For Christmas we had so much family over, pretty much all of my foster dad's side of the family including his parents, his brother and sister, brother in law and three nephews. It was a good weekend and the house was full. The boys (my younger cousins) were fun to hang out with and we went to the beach, where my uncle – who had the coolest hair- decided to get bogged a thousand times, and we all had a picnic. I had never had so much fun with a family like I did that day.

We went to bed Christmas eve and I woke up early. My stocking was full of so many presents and rolls of bubble wrap, because I told my new foster parents that I love bubble wrap, soon my foster dad's pa woke up and we had a very deep chat. He was a wise man and very factual. Soon everyone was up, and we had breakfast while I opened up my presents. I had 13 presents for the 13 years that I wasn't with them. I loved how much they wanted me to feel like I was home, and how they treat me like their daughter and not someone they were just fostering. Every time I would say that I was just their foster kid, they would tell me not to say the F word in the house. My new foster parents loved their gift and their letter. Baby B loved her gift too, which was a little car with wheels that she can ride around.

I got other gifts from so many family members and family friends of my new foster parents, who I had never met; but they still thought about me and wanted to get me something that made me feel like I mattered and was cared about. The only questioned I had was *why now? Why would someone see something special in me and see that I matter when no one else did?* I was confused and thought that surely they were faking because no one has ever been this kind to me.

After breakfast, I went to eldest sister and saw my nieces. There was my 6-year-old niece and my new niece who was born not too long before Christmas! Big sister was also there, and I had a second breakfast of bacon and eggs. We opened our presents and I stayed for a bit before I went and spent lunch with Hayley and Adam. I liked Hayley and Adam's new house, it was out of town and small, I got to see all their family again, some who I'd never met and some I had but hadn't seen for a while. It was good catching up with everyone and spending Christmas with those who were special to me.

Hayley and Adam use to live next to Mum and my sister, and I pretty much grew up around them they were like family – they still are. Before we got in to care we would go to their house hungry and in old torn clothes. If we were sick or had hurt ourselves they looked after us. Even while we were in care and we visited mum, we would go to their house. And to this day they have been close family friends and I know I can trust them with anything. They never judged me, and I enjoy being around them. It was special to have Christmas with them.

Once I got home it was fairly quiet. I rode my bike that I got from my new foster parents, hung out with my cousins and had some Aunty bonding time. Overall, surprisingly, it was a perfect Christmas. But like every Christmas, my room was a mess from all the presents and that was something I would have to deal with in the next few days

I remember when I was growing up Christmas was always good; it was good as a kid too. Mum was broke, but somehow we always got presents. While we were living with our first foster parents they always gave us good gifts. We were very fortunate and I'm grateful that even though I grew up in a bad place my mum and foster parents still tried giving me the best childhood. I just wish that it was a good childhood, but I'm a better person now for it.

After the Christmas rush we still had a few weeks before school starts, I used this time to hang with Baby B and have movie marathons. Georgia and I also hung out and did mini photoshoots and challenges which was fun. She had her birthday, which was a dinner, and that was a good night. However, earlier that day I had a fight with big sister which made me go home crying and my foster mum just held me and asked what happened. Other than that, I also got to see Lucy who I missed so much! The holidays were good and relaxing, but I started to fall back, and my anxiety rose which made my thoughts crazy and bad. I started to think that my new foster parents were going to give up on me and I started to shut down, something I did to protect myself.

I was diagnosed with anxiety, which apparently I had always had, but my mum self-diagnosed me with asthma, and if I wasn't having frequent panic attacks I wouldn't have known. My Foster mum and My Foster dad started making promises that they wouldn't give up and would always be my family. I would turn around and say 'don't make promises you can't keep,' but they were sure that they wouldn't break them. I didn't trust them, not when my life had been full of empty promises. Family had broken my heart before a boy ever had! So no matter how much I wanted to trust them, I couldn't. It was too hard... Soon enough our thing became 'always and forever.' If I was sad or scared and had fears they would always say 'always and forever.' Some days I believed them and some days I needed reassurance.

Baby B's birthday was in February and she turned one! She had grown so much, she was crawling, could say sissy and was so much cuter! Then around came March 11th – my birthday. I had made another milestone with my new family and that was amazing! I had two cheesecakes and had friends and family over. But big sister and mum didn't come. Big sister didn't, she made another excuse which made me upset, but eldest sister came so I got to see my nieces.

For my 15th birthday I wanted to do something special. I decided to do random acts of kindness, instead of making it about me – I wanted to help others. So some of my good friends and I got together and went around town. We handed out chocolates and compliments, it was a really good time. We had many people thank us and had businesses give us free chips or other stuff which was nice. We even made it on to Facebook and were again complimented. I wouldn't have wanted to spend my birthday any other way. It made me happy that I could do something nice, and in a way share God's light. Afterward, we went home and had a big sleepover.

That night was also the start of my journey on to medication for my depression and anxiety. The meds also helped with sleep, because I struggled so much to get to sleep. The first night I took them I was knocked out straight away. I was worried that the meds wouldn't work, and I hoped they did because I needed help. I didn't want to struggle anymore. In a way, even though it was my first night on medication, it was a really good day. I loved every bit of it, and I knew I wanted to do it again.

Before I knew it, it all started again – the suicidal thoughts, the self-harm and pushing everyone away. I was scared to lose my new family and I didn't know how to control my feelings or tell them, so I shut off completely and self-harmed. I was failing school and losing friends, I didn't want to live anymore, and it was getting too hard. I still had some good days, and spending time with Baby B made me happier. Even still, there were times when I would look at Baby B, maybe when I was feeding her a bottle or reading to her or letting her fall asleep in my arms, and ever so quietly I would tell her 'I'm sorry, you deserve a better sissy.'

Every week it was getting worse and I would try to hang myself or strangle myself with a cord in the hopes of passing out. Sometimes my foster mum or dad would come in and take it off me. It was scary, not just for me but for them too. I decided that I wanted to end my life, so I thought overdosing would work. I went to school as per usual, just before Easter, which I was keen about because of Easter Camp (but that's only if I didn't die). I wrote a letter for my new foster parents. Like always I took what I used to self-harm from school to home – I mostly self-harmed at school because that's where I was more stressed. And on a day when both my new foster parents had gone to work I opened my window, because I wasn't allowed to be home alone for obvious reasons.

I remember that day I had gotten into a disagreement with both of my new foster parents because I didn't want to go to school. Then I got upset, because arguing always makes me scared because I have a fear that they would get rid of me or that they would hit me. This made me realise I must've been hit as a kid because my new foster parents would never hurt me. Also, that was the day I had learned that my new foster parents had a cleaner come every few weeks, which I had no idea about because normally I clean the house. Especially when I've made them sad or when I was sad.

Once they went to work and I went on my bike, I rode around for a bit then I came back home. I took the screen off my window and opened it. Once inside, which was so much more intense than I thought, I went into my new foster parent's room, where they had all the medications, and I just grabbed whatever and left. I put the letter on my bed and quickly rode to the beach.

I grabbed some pills in my hand and took them, but within a minute or something I instantly regretted it. Something clicked in my mind – I don't know, I was scared, 'what if my new foster parents were actually get hurt by this?' I had so many questions. I messaged my foster mum what I had done, but she didn't reply. Out of fear I rode to the doctor's clinic where my foster mum worked and told the receptionist. My Foster mum, being a doctor, meant I had got to know everyone who worked in the clinic fairly well.

I waited in the waiting room and soon my doctor came out. I followed him into the room, and we talked. He was a pretty good doctor and when he wasn't my doctor, he was my uncle because my foster mum is half Asian and he was Asian. I went back into the waiting room and then I started to get really tired, I ended up sitting on the ground because I couldn't focus and wanted to sleep.

I was then called back into the room and this time I was snappy and angry, a thing that happens when I am tired. I asked him if he was even qualified which lead to a deep conversation. After everything, my foster mum and foster dad came, they weren't happy. I thought they hated me, and I was scared they didn't want me anymore. I had to have cords on me to check my heart.

After what felt like forever, I went home, and I wasn't allowed to go to my room so I went into the lounge room. I put my phone on charge and my foster mum walked in. She looked like she had either just cried or was about to cry, I hated seeing her upset and I hated myself for making her sad. They had done nothing but bring me into this family and I had treated them like this. She hugged me and started crying which made me cry. She said she was sorry and how she gotten off the phone with DCP. That scared me so much, what did they say? Am I leaving? She wouldn't tell me, but it played on my mind for ages.

I remember the first time my foster mum had cried in front of me and it was because I was suicidal. I remember her telling me that she loved me and doesn't want to lose me. But I didn't want to live anymore because I was scared, I was so scared. I just thought she was faking it, even though I knew you couldn't fake the care that was written all over her face.

My doctor came over after he finished work and cooked us dinner. It was amazing, it made me feel cared about knowing someone had gone far and beyond to genuinely give a shit. That night my foster mum came and hugged me. We started doing a night-time routine where my foster mum and dad would take it in turns spending time with me. Sometimes we would just talk, sometimes my foster mum would sing, and they would pray, and I would fall asleep. Some nights I couldn't sleep and would stay awake.

Finding a family like Mama and Daddo was good. I had a baby sister; my extended family was amazing and loved me, and didn't see me different; and Mama and my foster dad actually tried to be good parents – something I had never really had before. I felt at home, but I didn't know how to handle that. I had gone through home after home, I had to take care of myself and I was alone a lot. Now I had a home and a family. It was overwhelming and I didn't know how to cope with things from my past that had come to the surface – things that I didn't think even existed.

Some of the things that had come up were things like: if my foster dad had a beer and we had a disagreement, the smell of alcohol would flick something in my mind and instantly I would be fearful that he would hurt me. I couldn't tell him this though, because he was my dad and I knew that if I told him he would feel bad for something that happened to me when I was way too young to remember. Or sometimes I would be scared that I would wake up and it was all a dream, so this led to me being clingy like a little kid. I couldn't stop it because I had lost control of my thoughts and I needed to know they weren't leaving. If they left I would have a mental breakdown, it was tiring and draining on them, I could tell, but it was also just as bad on me.

I then started calling my foster dad 'Daddo' because he called me kiddo, so It was a perfect name. Or I would call him Poo Face because he calls me Poo Poo. My biological Dad had also decided to move closer to us girls to start a relationship with us, and I was excited to meet dad and get to know him. But after a while, all this hurt I had felt as a kid (that I pushed away) came up I got angry, but I didn't know how to cope. I never got taught how to cope with big feelings, so I took it out on Daddo. I was so upset I didn't want to be alone, but I also did want to be alone. I didn't want Daddo, but I wanted to be with Mama.

I would never hurt anyone, I am not that type of person, but I couldn't stop my sadness. One day, when things got quite intense, Mama and Baby B left for a walk. Knowing they had gone because of me made me hate myself and that only made me angrier. I had this thought that this was it – they would get rid of me for sure. With just my foster dad and I in the house, I went into the lounge room and collapsed on the ground I cried so much just saying over and over 'why did he leave?' My foster dad came in and just held me and I knew that this was what a dad was supposed to do. I had grown up being told by my family that Dad left because of me, and it affected me more than I knew.

But with everything happening, there was surprisingly some good. I had Easter Camp in a few days and wanted to go, Easter Camp was a special thing considering the year before when I went to camp I got to meet Mama and Daddo. At the time I hadn't known that that was the start of an amazing relationship and of course a new family.

Unfortunately, my social worker wasn't letting me go camping because I had tried to make myself overdose – I was so upset. I was looking forward to going to see Lucy and Georgia. Even Daddo and Mama weren't happy about me not being allowed to go to camp. Mama was going to take Georgia to camp – she was like my sister and she was part of the family. Daddo made phone call after phone call, telling them that I needed to go. After what felt like forever, finally, Daddo got it through to them and I was allowed to go. I was really grateful, and hugged Daddo saying thanks over and over again.

The camp was amazing, it went for four nights. But I went home on Sunday night after the family dinner. We had two good speakers, they both went through a lot growing up with drugs and they talked about stuff that I needed to hear. When we had quiet time, I would read my bible, talk to God and pray for others. I was so broken, to the point where I was in tears, I went on the beach, got on my knees, raised my arms to heaven and asked God to take it. Take all the pain *I want to follow you and trust you, but this is too hard and heavy* I cried out to him. And I felt like someone just took all the weight off me. I felt free and the were chains gone! God showed he was real, I knew he was, and he proved it again and again by answering my prayers for a family and protecting me. Now he had taken the chains off me – I was so happy.

I had some good chats with the speakers too, I told them about me, and they prayed for me. It was good to talk to someone. Some of the stuff they talked about in their sermons were things like: how trying to fit in isn't cool because we aren't called to fit in, and it doesn't get us anywhere, but giving our life to God gives us eternal life. Pride always comes before the fall! God is a cool guy and he wants us to be his friend, he is the only one who will save and give you life. God is always there, holding and loving us. The last bit really spoke to me, I had felt alone, lost and scared and being told that made me realise I'm not alone and God is holding me.

Once home from Camp I was in a better mood. I didn't feel depressed or suicidal, I was happy – I felt free and light. I focused on God and was doing better in school; it was my Easter Miracle and I thanked God every day for healing me. I don't know how I went from self-harm and suicidal actions to being happy and free. But here I am and for once I started to see things looking up. God had shown me over and over again that he was real, and he is loving and caring. He has blessed me over and over again.

With school I made new friends. I never had specific friends, I drifted from group to group. I guess in a way you could say I had friends but not best friends. I didn't have a friend I could turn to when I was faced with a problem. Though my problems are a bit too extreme to turn to a friend for, but mini problems like boys and homework is something I wish I had a friend for.

Mama was not just my mum, but also my best friend. I learned to trust her with my whole heart. I knew I could ask or tell her anything – she was the mum I had always wished I had. She was the mum everyone wants! With it being the new year, we had new people and new home groups. One new girl was really pretty, she was in a lot of my classes, but we didn't really talk much until one day when we were being stupid. There was this song that said something about 'the stone rolling away' so this girl and I would go around saying 'and the stone rolllllleddd away.' We weren't friends, but we talked a bit in classes.

In one class we had to do a dot-to-dot drawing, just like in year 1! This class was fun, it was called STEM and we would do Math and science and that stuff. So I sat with her and that was the start of our friendship. I was glad I had found a friend, we got along well. We also had another friend (who had been kind of my friend before) and then had another girl as well, so it was us four. We were that crazy group of friends, we did everything together – even our group projects. I loved having a group like them, I don't think the teachers enjoyed it, but we only had a few years left of school.

We did concentrate and did our work, and had the best sleepovers. They are great friends and I couldn't have asked for better, but that's not saying I didn't have Lucy and Georgia – they are incredible and like family, but it was also good having friends in school who I could have sleep-overs with.

Some days I wished it was only issues with friends that I had, because friendship issues are easier than family issues. Growing up I had lots of friendship issues and had my fair share of being bullied and bullying. I now hate that I bullied others out of my pain, even now I get bullied, so I retaliate and bully back. When I was a kid, I even went to counselling through 'Child and Adolescent Mental Health service', (CAMHS), maybe that's where my hate for it started. But now that I am older, I realised that friendship issues aren't that bad. I think it's easier to cope with than having issues with family.

Unfortunately, I had a different type of family. One day they are supportive and loving and the next they were mean and toxic, and it drained me and took a toll on my mental health, which I took out on Mama and Daddo, and I hate that. I trust my counsellor and tell her everything in the hopes that I would be able to change, learn to cope and talk about my problems in a good way. Instead I cry and have a breakdown, and at one point I want Mama and Daddo, then I don't want them (but I do) and it's hard. And no doubt it was hard for Mama and Daddo too, it would be hard on anyone having a child who didn't know how to express their emotions or talk about it but would instead have breakdowns. Part of me knew it wasn't my fault, I had faced a lot of rejections and pain from others and been silenced about how I felt. I couldn't help it, but another part of me blamed myself for it all, because if this happened over and over again then that meant something was wrong with me. I would rather blame myself its easier that way.

It sucked, big sister and I were on and off. We got along and then she would go bad and would tell me to die or swear at me and say 'you are not my sister.' It really hurt me, but I coped, I was glad I had Mama and Daddo there with me holding me. I think my Dad was a bit jealous, even though he had just come into my life. He thought that he could come into my life and be a Dad, but he didn't realise that he had hurt me and couldn't just waltz in, so that made it hard. Then eldest sister was good, but she didn't want me to talk to big sister, otherwise she would cut me out, but when she wants to be she is the best support.

There were times when I wanted to cut them out because they weren't helping my mental and emotional wellbeing, but I was scared about what they would say behind my back, so I stuck through. It was hard trying to explain to Mama and Daddo that cutting them out was easier and healthier. I learned that Mama and Daddo they think talking it through would help because they see the best in people which is something I love about them. But it also annoyed me because my biological family are shitty; they don't talk things through, they all want to be the victim, and they won't fix things.

Its draining trying to talk to them because straight away it's an argument.

One morning I had disagreed with Mama and Daddo the night before. Tt was more the fact that I had had a bad day, so I didn't want to be alone, because night time is when I struggled the most. My thoughts are wild and scary, so I was a mess begging them to stay. In the end, I cried myself to sleep, woke up early and eldest sister had messaged me – we had an argument. I cried so much I couldn't deal with it anymore, I was going to the lounge room, because I wanted to lay on the couch before everyone woke up and cry, but as I left my room Mama was coming out of Baby B's room. She hugged me and kissed my cheek and I said probably the stupidest thing: 'how's my tear-stained face?' not thinking about the night before. I didn't realise until the next moment why she got upset at what I said and walked away. I realised she must've thought I meant about how I had cried after our chat last night.

A few minutes later she came into the lounge room and I told her I was sorry, how I hadn't mean it like that, and I told her what happened and started crying. She then said sorry for assuming and all was well, she just sat there holding me as I cried. I wished my family was this nice and loving, it was going to hurt so much if I leave because this is the one family I love. They are a real family, even if that offends my biological family, I don't mind. They had my whole life to be a good family, and Mama and Daddo stepped up and made up for the years where I didn't have anyone. So they can't blame me for being closer to and seeing Mama and Daddo as my real family. Being at home has taught me how truly broken my family was and how much they hurt me. Yes, every family has their flaws, but none like mine and I'm glad I learned how much they hurt me, but I am also sad that I never had a good family until Mama and Daddo.

A couple of months after Easter, what I like to call my Easter Miracle, went well. I mean there were days where I was very happy, I felt free and safe, finally safe, but there were days where I thought I wouldn't ever have a happy ending and thought suicide was the only option. I had never felt this safe and I guess I wasn't used to this, so it was overwhelming and every time they promised to not give up on me, and every time they spoiled me, stood up for me, or were just good parents and loved me, I didn't know how to cope or what to do and I pushed them away. In a way, I thought it was easier if I gave up before they could give up on me.

I felt like a horrible daughter because of the amount of times Daddo walked into my room having and had to take things off me when I was trying to hurt myself; or when I would look into Mama's eyes and see the pain and fear. I knew she wanted to take the pain away from me and was scared of losing me. Bedtimes were when I got to spend time with Mama, and I liked looking up at her. They say you know when someone lies because they can't hide their emotions in their eyes, eyes hold lots of emotions and tell their own story.

When I looked up at her eyes, I could see that she really did love me and saw me as her daughter, so why was I determined to die? Maybe it's because I knew I was a monster who destroyed everything, and I couldn't let them be someone I destroyed – not this family. I didn't want to hurt them, and I guess I thought if I died they wouldn't hurt as much because I had only been there for eight months so they wouldn't care as much. But looking up at her I knew it would kill her. I was torn, emotionally drained and a mess. I had messed up already when I was upset. I changed and I cried, and I didn't want to be alone, whereas when I was happy I felt like I belonged. I didn't see why they still stuck around, but I wanted to focus on being in this family.

I trusted them with all my heart. I told them my darkest secrets and fears, even that didn't make them leave, so could this be the final move. I sure hope so. I was failing school, but I tried to do my best. Sometimes it got stressful and it made me self-harm. I didn't do it much at home, mainly at school which no one noticed so it was good (sometimes they did but they couldn't stop me). It was nearly the holidays which was a plus, I got to be home with Baby B, playing with her and she was growing way too fast. It was sad, but I loved being a part of her, like watching her grow.

We also had this random person coming over who was staying for a while. It was a student doctor apparently, she was staying with someone else but was coming over for dinner and stuff with us. I am a shy person when you first meet me and once thing I had learned about this family was that Mama and Daddo knew so many people. The first night she came I was outside putting clothes on the line, because I was a good daughter and did chores – especially washing the dishes, mainly when I was sad, or Mama was on call. I wanted to clean for them, but my room was barely clean so there was that.

Anyway, as I was hanging the clothes, I heard them welcoming the visitors. Typical me hid out the back whilst trying to see what she looked like. I mean I would have to cope with a random for like a month, they better be nice, but I do trust Mama and Daddo's choice of friends so meh. I realised I couldn't hide all night and I actually had to talk to this person like the good girl I was.

'who at first, I thought was her husband, until I realised she was a lot younger than him. After what felt like years, I found out he was her dad.' That night was the start of some amazing nights. She actually seemed cool, but I wouldn't tell her that. Instead I pulled out the 'I will send you to Egypt and put you in a pyramid,' and other sarcastic remarks. She was funny, and we got along and I thought *hey this Kayla chick is kind of cool*. We also had a massive debate because she had a purple stethoscope which to her was blue, so we went so far as to try and win the debate. We got all the doctors involved, our social media friends, everyone. It was really fun, and we went to the beach and had photoshoots.

We grew close and she gave pretty good hugs and had some embarrassing stories that I would forever use against her. It was fun to have someone to be sarcastic with and be stupid, I wasn't so sad but happy and looked forward to hanging with her most days and couldn't wait to beat her in our debates. Some other exciting stuff was that Georgia and I were getting ready for a trip to the big city, to a youth conference. I haven't been to one for about year and was super excited. It was my first flight alone (though I had Georgia) and it was time I got to spend with my best friend and God.

With excitement we packed and were waiting to finally go to the big city. I was going to miss the fam. Before we left, we had a mini birthday party for Mama, I made her favourite cake – black forest – and I put Oreo pieces with lolly snakes inside and on top it said 'older than dirt.' I had to say Pinterest never disappoints. I also bought her favourite chocolate and 'open when cards'. I was going to write one for a just in case I had to move out but I decided against it. I got her some other stuff too.

I think I am pretty good at planning parties. Daddo's birthday was May the 4th (and yes, he is obsessed with Star Wars!) So we decided to throw him a massive surprise party that was Star Wars themed and it was pretty good. He LOVED it! We even had some people come and dress up as Darth Vada. I had fun planning it with Mama. We had balloons and a homemade photo booth, cake and dressed up as a character from Star Wars. At that point I had never watched it, I thought it would be boring. Only a couple of months after did I decide to watch it and it was as bad as I thought.

Well it was time for our little trip to the big city and we both were pumped. I was going to miss my family, I hated being away from them, fear of it all being a dream and that they would leave I guess. I also started getting what was kind of like separation anxiety, I didn't like being away from home, but whenever I went away we would call each other. And as someone who hates flying, I was not looking forward to the flight, I loved the prettiness – it was the turbulence that I hated. The sky looked good and the weather was nice, so I didn't think there was going to be any issues, which was good.

On the flight we were pretty much at the front of the plane, I put my earphones in watching a Netflix show I had already downloaded before to try to block out the loud engine that was deafening. The 45 minutes were quick. I was messing around with Georgia, pretending the plane was about to crash and making the flight attendant laugh at us and I even danced a little bit (obviously in my seat). I was embarrassing Georgia, not myself! Once on land, we waited for Daddo's mum (Gran) to pick us up because we were staying with her while we were away, which was going to be a good time. After Gran picked us up, we went to the mall, we arrived at a good time as there were sales. It was great, we got lots of clothes and treated ourselves. Once we had done that we arrived home to get ready for our first night of the conference.

Like any church event, I got dressed up. Growing up in a strict Christian home it had been drilled into my brain that I need to go to church looking nice and pretty. Once I said 'I don't think God cares how I look, he loves me how I am.' Oh boy, was I wrong. My foster mum told me 'he does care, and you need to be respectful.' I quickly shut my mouth knowing it was best to not argue back. The first night was amazing, the church was Mama and Daddo's church before they moved down to our little town we call home. And because Mama and Daddo are well known and loved, (and they liked telling everyone about me, why?) I will never know but something in me told me to trust them so I did.

Arriving at the building, lots of people came and said hi, introducing themselves. Some people were excited to meet me finally, so I was hugged a lot. It was good meeting all the people that Mama and Daddo know and love. They seemed nice and the senior pastors were pretty cool, I was glad that I had people who I had never met love, support and pray for me. We sang worship songs, one thing I loved about church and the conference is worshiping with Georgia. She hasn't had it easy and I am so glad that I could be on the journey with her, l loved seeing people come to God and she had come so far. After a bit of worship, we all took our seats and had a few games. Then it was time for the speakers, one of the them was one of my favourite speakers, he came a few years back and spoke at a youth event at home and it is hilarious. It was the same for the next couple of days, it was full days for about two days with songs, tears, workshops, lessons and prayers. On the last day of the conference we had so many jumping castles and music battles, it was an amazing getaway.

I even had some pretty good conversations with some people, one of the leaders came up to me and we chatted. We talked about life and I told her a bit about me, 'I saw how you worship, I love how you worship,' she complimented. 'Aw thanks, yes I give my life to God. I seriously don't know what I would do without him or where I would be, I love him so much. He has been here for me when I had no one,' I replied honestly, because God is my everything – he did create me, so he is a part of me and always will be.

I grew so close to God and learned so much, once the conference was done, I thought about all I had learned from my speakers. I learned that God makes somebodies out of nobodies, when others see no worth God see worth and helps us become amazing people. And how he calls us to make a difference to those around us, that we shouldn't live like a trend come one minute gone the next and living for short term excitement, but instead live for him bring others to him. One of our speakers talked about the importance of being different. He said we shouldn't be like M&M's, which are the same as all the others in a pack and go unnoticed when they are gone. Instead we should be like a chocolate bar whose absence is noted. This is how we should transform our lives. I also learned the difference between a solider and a warrior, and how we should be warriors who get given a task and achieve it. We should have the same mindset as God.

Another thing I learned was how we shouldn't worry about the voices around us, and how we need to turn our focus on God. We should listen to him, not the voices that say we are nobodies. Some other things were that the Enemy has a problem and we are that problem, he doesn't want us to follow God and when we do, we defeat him. And if we don't quit, we don't fail, so if we don't want fail then we should never quit.

I still had a couple of days before going home, which I spent with my other set of grandparents. One night Georgia went out, so I went to Ardy and Lizzy's which was the second time I had been over - my first time was at the start of the year, I had bad stomach pain and had to have a surgery to take my appendix out. It was my first big surgery and I was scared but Mama and Daddo were there holding my hand. I nearly cried getting wheeled to the surgery room, because there was a point where Daddo had left but I put on a brave face, smiled and focused on God knowing he would take care of me. The nurses were sweet.

The next day we went to the big city and I remembered how when I was coming out of the operation, I touched my unbrushed hair and said 'oh, that's so nice they braided my hair for me.' Yeah, because while cutting me open they thought it would be nice to braid my hair. It made me feel so embarrassed. So, we went to the big city and I had to rest, I was so overtired and emotional and I got snappy with Mama and Daddo.

One of the nights I went over to Ardy and Lizzy's and it was the night of the royal wedding, something that had my care factor at a zero, but Lizzy loved it and to be fair I did entertain myself by making fun of it and being typical me. After spending time with them I went home and then the Saturday, the day before I was supposed to go home, Grandma (Mama's mum) took me on a special, horse ride for quality times. It was probably one of my favourite things about my time away. I may live in the country, but I don't get to go horse riding or trail riding much so this was INCREDIBLE. I loved it.

Sunday, before we went home, we went to the church where the conference was and I got to meet Mama's best friend and some other people, which was nice. But like all good things, it must come to an end. So on the plane we got, and 45 minutes later we arrived home. We had a welcome home dinner which was nice and got ready for school and hopefully no mental health crashes.

It was coming up to September and it had nearly been a whole year being with this family, (my second longest placement so far). It was good, I mean we did have ups and downs sometimes. I had really bad episodes and became suicidal or clingy because I was scared of being alone. It was almost like I wasn't in control of myself which scared me so much. I knew it was taking a toll on them as well. In the end, they were getting drained and tired, so I went in to Respite, which I hated because every respite trip had always ended up with my placement ending. So whenever I went away (normally to my sisters) I would have a breakdown because I was so scared. But I rang them every night, some nights I cried to them, worried they were going to leave.

It felt like they were evaporating out of my hands and moving off into the distance. It was like I was reaching out but couldn't reach them which is what I feared. About halfway through September, I had a particularly hard night, no surprise. But it was also one of the most powerful nights I had had in my life. It started as some cuddles on the couch while listening to some worship. We were praying in tongues, something I grew up knowing as my first foster parents were pastors and had that spiritual gift. Growing up I was fascinated by it, most kids would think it's weird and abnormal, but I thought it was incredible. It was something I have always wanted and prayed about. So when we prayed I was not weirded out, instead it was calming and I felt a peace. I felt safe, like God himself was there holding me, not my Mama

I knew I was ready to ask the Holy Spirit to feel me, to give me this extraordinarily powerful gift. There's something about the spiritual world that as humans we don't understand. It was too big for us to wrap our heads around. Not only was it calming when she prayed in the spirit, but every now and then I would have like a panic attack. I was shaking and I focused on her voice. But this wasn't anxiety, this was spiritual, and I focused on the music trying to calm myself. Baby B was crying so both Mama and Daddo went to check on her. While they were away I said a quick prayer asking God for the gift of the spirit.

And those simple words were all it took, and I don't know how to explain it I felt at peace, but there was something different. I had an urge to say something out loud but the words weren't coming out, well not English anyway. It was words I didn't even understand, but I felt like I had to say them and when I did at first it was weird, but I felt calm, safe and peaceful. I didn't know if it was really the spirit working in me or what, but I trusted God. Once they came back, I told her what had happened, and she was really happy I had received the gift, but I didn't know if it really was the gift of the spirit or not.

To end the night, they prayed over my room, prayed that any evil spirit that was in my room would leave. Prayed that Jesus would protect my room and me too. Unfortunately, that only lasted a couple of days, I guess I wasn't trusting God or praying, I had the family I needed, and I guess I pushed him away – why do I need him? I didn't know how much I needed him. I still prayed… sometimes, and that night wasn't made up. Whenever I prayed the holy spirit would take over and speak words for me, I didn't understand it all but I knew I didn't have to because God understood. I could go weeks without praying and without thinking those words would come out something – I couldn't make up.

My mental health started to get bad, there were nights where I wanted to kill myself. I tried a lot, but I didn't want to die, I just wanted to pain to end. I was so happy in this family, so I didn't understand why I was feeling like this. It was like I could only be happy for a couple of weeks and then I would be back to square one. I was tired of fighting to be happy, only for it to last for a short while. It good so bad that a few times I had to have some trips to the hospital and spend a night.

I was scared of losing myself again, I didn't think anyone needed me – not as much as I needed them. But truth be told, I didn't need people I needed God. But I kept him at arm's reach. I still went to church, but I was such a hypocrite telling all my friends they need to trust God and pray and I wasn't doing the same.

One night, I wouldn't say I got into an argument with Daddo, but I was a mess. I wanted Mama, but she was asleep and he was there. I was crying and I pushed him away. He was trying so, so hard to be there, to hold me as I cried, to protect me. I didn't want him to be there, but in the same way I did, and I was confused. In the end, he was so worn out I ended needing to go to the hospital. I didn't want to go, and I hated myself. Oh I was so mad at myself.

I went into the ambulance and the police from my hometown came up to make sure I went. He was my dance teacher's husband and he is a great guy. He talked to me while I was crying and then he prayed. Daddo was there with me, he was the best dad ever so why was I hurting him? He wasn't the one who walked, who gave up on me, who didn't contact me for years. Sitting here was a father that had fought for me, loved me, and would do anything to keep me safe.

I was in hospital for a few nights and I was alone some days. Some days Mama and Daddo came some days they didn't. I played games, cried, prayed and watched Tv. Gran (Daddo's mum) came and that same day I had to go into respite care. I was so numb, no emotions came to me, was this the end? Had they finally given up? They said I would only be there for a week, I hoped so.

Every couple of days I saw them and Baby B, which was good because I missed them. I missed them so much. They did talk to me as though they there could be a chance that I wouldn't come home and this scared me. So, I decided if I got my life together, if I became close to God, I could change and they would bring me back home. Every day I prayed, read my bible, but there was something inside me that knew that this wasn't going to bring me back home. I had messed up and this is what I would have to live with. But I kept fighting and tried to convince them I was better, tried to convince myself I would be back home, fooling myself.

And then the day came what I was dreading for a whole year. It was a message that Mama had sent it was her telling me It wasn't working, they were drained and tired. They were struggling the marriage and their own family was on the line. It was like I was a toxic disease, not that they implied it, but I felt it.

When I read that message all the colour left my face as fast as anything, I was numbed. My legs felt like they were going to give way. My heart – my heart felt like someone went, got a hammer and smashed it to pieces. I felt like I was in a slow-motion movie, like someone had died. I swear a part of me had. Wasn't I enough? *God why did you leave me again?* I cried out, though I knew he didn't plan this. I tried everything but it was no use.

I didn't just break me, it broke them. I had destroyed them! One of the times I hung with them after the message Mama was crying – I had never seen her cry so much. Daddo's eyes had begun to water. They didn't want this to happen and I knew they didn't have a choice. I could never blame them, no matter how much it had broken me. One time Mama told me that it hurt a lot and I had never heard anything I could relate to so much.

When I had moved into this home, I knew it was going to hurt and that it was going to destroy me. They said sorry so much, and it hurt to see them hurt. I felt like the worst person ever. I had never hated anyone as much as I hated myself. But they promised they would always be my parents and my family, even though it looked different. I wanted to trust them, but I knew it could only take time.

They rang me every night, some night just like when I lived at home, I would begging them to take me home. I had wanted a family for so long, but had just come and gone so fast and I took so much for granted. I knew begging wasn't going to do anything, but I had to try. I cried myself to sleep so much after leaving. I cried more than ever. I cried until there were no tears, left until my eyes stung.

The hardest thing that they had to do was let me go to keep me safe. The hardest thing for me to do was accept that and learn to cope. To get used to it, to trust God and have faith that he was working in this family. To be a better person and focus on what good could come out of this, if anything good could come out of it.

Part Four

TRIAL INTO TRIUMPH.

'Only God can turn a mess into a message and worrier into a warrior, a test into a testimony and a trial into a triumph.'

~ UNKNOWN

After I left home, DCP decided that it would be a good idea to make me move schools. I didn't get a choice at all and I wasn't happy. I didn't even get to say goodbye to anyone at school. I had a lot of troubles at the school, but I also had lots of support. I spent so much of my life letting people control it and make choices thinking they knew what was best for me. As a child I could understand why they would be controlling my life, but when I left my first foster carers I was no longer happy about DCP controlling my life.

Now, I know that I was 14 and wasn't mature enough emotionally or mentally to make decisions for myself. But as a teenager, who is nearly 16, I knew better than anyone else about what was best for me and my health, and what would help me become a better person. I just hoped and prayed that my new school was going to be the new fresh start that I needed. When I went for the school tour, I went with eldest sister because I didn't want to go with my caseworker. At my old school we judged this school, but in doing the tour I found there were some aspects in this new school that were better. The principal was nice as well, I was starting at the end of the week and was nervous. I didn't want to be at a new school without my new foster parents. I didn't want to do anything without them.

They were the only parents who I felt like were like my parents and I hated myself for letting them down. I knew that people weren't ours to have, so I had to put my trust in God. This year I had grown so much, I grew closer to God every day. I had moved out of home, the home I knew in my heart would always be my home no matter where I was. After moving out I had a week where I prayed and read the bible like it was my lifeline. In a way, God is my lifeline. I needed him like I needed air, so as I was praying and spending every day with God, I realised something.

When I was living at home and grew closer with Mama and Daddo, I had started pushing God away. Yes, I grew closer to God, but I grew as close as I could with a barrier that I held up. When things went well I thanked God, but when things went bad, I tried get healing from Mama and Daddo. I almost expected them to fix me and so I kept pushing God away and putting them first – not God. When I realised that, I felt so bad. I said sorry to God and asked for forgiveness. I told God that I was now always going to put him first.

I knew that I wasn't going back home and had to learn to do it alone. It was going to be hard but there wasn't much I could do. That week was a powerful week, I grew closer to God and I didn't think it could be possible. As the week went by, it was finally my first day at my new school. I was nervous, it had been a long time since I was the 'new kid'. I walked into the school knowing that I couldn't go through school with friends. I didn't want friends, because I wanted to get my schooling over and done with. I had way too much stress to deal with friendship drama, so I decided it was for the best that I didn't have friends through school. But I still had Lucy and Georgia and my youth outside of school, and friends from navigator's, so I didn't fully isolate myself.

The first day went by fairly quickly. I met my class and teachers, and when I got home I saw a bouquet of flowers on the bench and there was a card for yours truly.... ME. Of course a guy didn't get them for me, because that only happens in movies. I read the card and it was from my family back home. I typed my mama a quick thankyou and put them in my room. The first two days of school went quickly, and the weekend came.

Mama, Daddo and my baby sister went to Adelaide, to Ardy Pa's and Nans river house. I was still a bit sad that I couldn't go. I didn't ring them while they were away or message them much because it was their break to grieve and a time for me to grieve too. I was still a mess after leaving and wished I was home.

Mama and Daddo knew that fear, I know they hadn't wanted it to go this way. But it did nothing but prove that respite in fact does lead to placement ending. In the end, it wasn't their fault but it did show how messed up broken I was. I didn't start school off well, I skipped a bit and stayed home but I didn't care. It was my new school, I didn't have a home and I was struggling so I didn't care if I was at school or not. In my first couple of weeks I sat with everyone at recess and lunch, even though I didn't want friends. They had invited me to sit with them, so I did. Before I knew it, it was our one-year family anniversary. Some people thought it was weird that I didn't live with them but still called them Mama and Daddo, and that they wanted me to be their daughter. I didn't care what they thought.

Mama and my Baby B picked me up and we went home together to get ready for eldest sister to do our family photoshoot. I got to spend half the day with them, and it was good to be home, but there was a part of me that was pained and wished that I could've stayed. After our shoot, we had dinner which was one of my many favourite meals…. Okonomiyaki and fried rice. After dinner I went into what was once my room, though it looked untouched. I knew in a few weeks it would be back to a guest room. I pulled down my memory box and looked through it as stray tears spilled. I knew I nearly lost the one thing that my heart had longed for for all those years… parents who loved me.

I am so glad they still wanted me to be their daughter, I don't know what I would've done otherwise. Mama came into my room and we laid on my bed cuddling like the old times. I didn't want to let go, I wanted to wake up from this nightmare. Unfortunately, the time to leave came far too quick and before I knew it I was driving away from a place I didn't think I would ever have to leave (not until Uni anyway). The past two weeks had been really hard, I had moved from the house that felt like home, then I was moved to a new school where I didn't know anyone.

I once again got called by DCP and was informed that I had a new home and I was moving in at the end of the week. Funnily enough, I knew the couple. I had known them for years they were friends of my Mum. I was a bit happy that I could give this family life one more go, and if it didn't work then I knew I would be better off living alone and being independent. Independent living is for teenagers at the ages of 16 and up (which for me would be 5ish months), who can't live at home for any reason. Instead they lived in their own house with the help of the company who ran the housing for teens. But I didn't have to think about that yet, but of course I did have my concerns. I had just left a placement that lasted close to a year, it was the only placement that I had felt like I belonged, felt loved and for the first time in my life I was WANTED!

I was happy about having a new home, but to be honest I was kind of pissed (excuse my French) because it had only been a month and I hadn't even had time to grieve or process anything that had happened. But of course, DCP didn't care about all that it, almost feels like us foster kids aren't even human to them. We are just kids who have no feelings or emotions and just need a home. As long as we were placed in a house it's all good and less paperwork for them. Just like how some carers only are foster parents for money, so what does that make us kids? Yep, that's right, money makers. In a week I would be starting everything again, but I was glad that I knew them because I was a bit more comfortable. The week couldn't go any slower, the week was pretty much full of arguments between me and the carer I was with. We would argue a lot, but of course we got along sometimes too. I was grateful for her letting me stay, but I was so focused on the pain I was going through which made me snap easily.

I was forever grateful for Georgia, my best friend. We always talked on the phone and we had some very interesting conversations, but thanks to her the pain I had gone through was a bit more bearable. In the end it wasn't only hard on me, Mama and Daddo, but also on Georgia. We were together pretty much every day, we did everything together and we were like sisters. So our phone calls, in a way, helped us both no matter how strange our calls were. Near the end of the week, I was half packed and the carer I stayed with had gotten me a gift. It was a pineapple necklace, because everyone knows I loved pineapple. But I didn't really want to walk around with a necklace that was a pineapple, I wasn't that obsessed, so I said thank you, got home and put it on my desk.

Thursday night I got into an argument about God knows what with the carer, so I went to bed. I contemplated killing myself, not because of the fight but just everything had come bubbling up. The past couple of weeks were hard, I blamed myself for failing Mama and for being the reason why I didn't have a family. I was a mess, I could barely have a normal phone call with Mama and Daddo without being a mess. I was a crappy person and I felt horrible. I hadn't made them proud and I needed this time to make them proud. A part of me thought that if I grew closer to God, and became less depressed, maybe they would have me back. Another part of me knew that it wouldn't happen. I cried myself to sleep and before I knew it, it was Friday. I was not in the mood to go to school, so instead I got into an argument yet again. Once she went to work I messaged my caseworker and asked her if it was possible to move earlier, because I was supposed to move after school. She replied and said I can move to my new home around 11.

I packed my remaining stuff and put them all by the door. I had so many bags. I was sitting on a chair and eating a snack, and as I got up the seat broke. The seats were very wobbly so I wasn't shocked. I was worried though, because I knew she would probably try to say I did it on purpose. So when my worker picked me up and helped me with my stuff, I told her what had happened, and she said it would be okay. When we arrived at my new house it was awkward at first becasue she was overly excited. I, on the other hand, had trouble showing my emotions which meant on the outside I probably didn't look excited or happy, even though I was.

After a while my worker said goodbye and left, so I went into my room and put my stuff away. I left a path for me to get out the door and back to my bed because I knew it would take a while to unpack. The house was beautiful, My bedroom wasn't big or small; I had a double sized bed and mirror and lots of cupboard space. I had my own bathroom and I was in awe when I saw it. The bathroom was a shower and spa-like bath, with nice marble benchtops. I also had a toilet next door to the bathroom. The house was big for a couple who had kids that had left home, but I liked it. They also had a little black dog, who was adorable, and a cat.

My first week at my new home went well. I had finally unpacked everything and it took a lot of self-persuasion because I was cautious about it – worried that they would give up on me after a week or so. But I tried having faith that this would work out. I regularly saw

Mama and Daddo and my baby sister, I also texted them and rang them. School was alright, people stilled tried to be my friend, but I really didn't want to be friends with anyone. I just needed to get through school, get a good career and make a family that I would never give up on so that I could raise my kids to have the life I wish I had. Having anxiety, I was always planning my future so I could have something to look forward to, but also because I was worried that if I didn't have a plan my future would be bad. After a while, my caseworker stopped asking me how I was, was I surprised? Not at all, there was a part of me that was glad, but a bit that wished she would do her job and check in on me.

It was hard being away from home, I may only have been there for a year, but it was the only place that really felt like home. I had never fully grieved and I couldn't look at our family photo that was in my room without either crying or blaming myself. In the end I couldn't stand looking at it, so I put face down on my dresser. Our phone calls were good, but I missed them, I needed to be in my parents' arms. When you find the one thing your heart has longed for for so long, you are happy. But when it gets taken away you are a mess because after such a long time you had found that love, or that thing you didn't get as a kid, and it's hard to let it go again. After a while my new carers didn't like the fact that I was still talking to them or seeing them. They would say hurtful things, like that they didn't want me, and that they gave up on me. Or that they weren't my parents anymore and I knew it was probably their way of protecting me, but I was scared that I would get hurt again.

Hearing those words again cut deep for me, because I was already having those bad thoughts and I didn't need to go through it daily. We argued so much, I didn't like it and I had nowhere to turn. Even school got hard, so I skipped. I didn't purposely get into trouble, but I was always yelled at for something. Church and youth became my escape, those two things and my counsellor were the only things/people that had never left me and were there for me.

By my second week of living there I was so angry and upset that I decided I needed to escape life. I took my antidepressants but I knew I didn't take enough, and I started cutting – something I wish I had never started. When I finally came to my senses, I knew what I did was stupid, so I messaged the only person I wanted at that moment – my Mama. She told me to tell my carer and I did it but didn't go well. She said it was nothing, that I would be fine and that I was doing it for attention. I was shocked. I didn't do it for attention but there was a part of me that wished she showed she cared. After that, I didn't really talk to her and I kept things to myself. Well me and my pins – the one thing that was my pain relief. My carer would sometimes tell me she was going to tell DCP, to stop contact between Mama and Daddo. I knew if I said anything she would deny it so I kept it to myself.

One day we were at the doctors (my therapist) and I said I wanted to go alone because I didn't want her to come in as I had some issues that I wanted to talk about privately. Our chat was good, I enjoyed being sassy and he would always joke around with me. Some days I didn't like him but some days he was fun and easy to talk to. When I walked out, I saw my Mama, we talked and hugged before I departed. In the car, all hell broke loose because she was angry that she drove me up to Tumby only to sit waiting for me. She had wanted to be part of the session. After a bit, I got sick of it, so I messaged Georgia telling her that I'm about to ring her and why. The rest of the drive I was on the phone to my best friend.

When we had nearly arrived at Lincoln my carer said how she was going to go to DCP and tell them to stop all contact. Georgia, being the protective friend she is, heard it and she was not happy – Luckily she was not on speaker. Once home, I went into my room not wanting anything to do with her. I decided I didn't want to go to school on the last two days of the week, and because of my mental health I wasn't allowed to stay home, so I went into their work with them. I was then told by Mama that they wanted to pull back on contact. I was only allowed to call once a week, but I could message whenever. It wasn't the contact change that made me upset, it was the feeling that it wasn't their choice. Maybe it was the paranoia from what my carer said day in and day out, but no matter how much Mama told me it was what they had decided I still didn't believe them.

So I was annoyed and it was made worse when my caseworker came in because we had a heated argument. After a hectic week, I needed to do some more after school activities. I did dance and that was good. But I decided I wanted to learn more guitar, so I started go to music practice for church. The first night was great, I learnt a lot and had fun. Once everyone else had left I got talking with the music coordinator Ben, and his wife Ana. I let them in little by little, they told me how they remembered the day I was in front of church talking about conference – that was a year ago. I was surprised they, or anyone, remembered that. After a while I said goodbye, hugged them and said thanks. I was glad that I had something other than dance to look forward to, and slowly but surely my support circle was growing. By week three of having a new home there wasn't a day that wasn't full of arguments.

There was one good day, when my carer and I went for a drive to Whyalla and her husband stayed home. Whyalla was about a three-hour drive from Port Lincoln. Port Lincoln was an isolated place; the two closest towns are about 45 minutes. The drive was good, I always had loved long drives, and the drive was full of singing. Even though it was good, the drive gave me a lot of time to think. The past month was hectic, I had left a home that I missed, and I missed my Mama's loving arms and the safety of a father's love. I hadn't really given myself time to grieve and being in this new home was tense. I felt like I was expected to move on straightaway. With other families it was easy to move on quickly because I was either not there longer enough or because I had never had that strong parent daughter relationship/connection. So I let my tears run freely and it was lucky I was a silent crier (sometimes), so I was able to sing along to battle scars and cry. We had gone to Whyalla for a baby shower but I don't like big crowds because after a while it gets too overwhelming and I have to leave. After a couple of hours for cake and lunch we got up and left. Unsurprisingly on the drive back I again cried.

I still classified it as a good day because I finally started to realise that it's actually good to let the tears out. Music practice and dance was also good and the dance concert was fast approaching. I was excited but also sad because I didn't have my family coming to watch me. Ash was always supportive, and I couldn't ask for better support or dance teacher. Music was a good escape and I grew closer to Ana, more so then Ben, but I was thankful for them both. I also saw my counsellor every week and I was glad I still had her as a big support; even if there were days where I wished I stopped seeing her for my own pride because I wanted to do it alone with my own strength. On our second-to-last practice at the theatre before our dance concert, I started getting along with my sometimes-arch-enemy who was a girl I went to school with we were friends then bullies and because we did dance we tried to get along It was also Halloween and we wanted to all hang out. I had grown up in strict Christian homes so that meant no Halloween. For once, I wanted to just be like everyone else and I needed a girls' night out. We had fun, it was us two girls and few boys, we got a lot of lollies and chocolate. We even went to a dodgy house and got offered a bong: #nothanks.

Going out involved lots of convincing and a curfew of 7:30pm. Did I get home at 7:30? No, but in my defence my phone had gone flat and all my friends left, so I went to Foster carer'ss. I was in the area and I didn't know who else to go to. Once my phone was charged, I saw lots of missed calls, and after a while I got picked up. Let me just say the drive back wasn't pleasant. We argued, I tried to say sorry and explain but it didn't work. I kind of understood because it was her husband's birthday.

The week was uneventful, but Saturday came and the day started off bad. I am a hot sleeper, so sometimes I will just be in a bra and underwear, then in comes my foster mum and she is yelling about who knows what, pulls my cover off and tells me to get out of bed. *Someone woke up on the wrong side of the bed*, I thought to myself. I had dance and I decided to hang out with a few of the girls, oh what fun that was. First, was when I had a pillowcase of clothes for dance practise, so I wanted to drop it off at their work. I saw my foster carer's car so I yelled at them to wait, she looked at me and started driving. So I chased after her, but she sped off. I tried ringing her, but she wouldn't answer. We then walked around the street having fun, I must admit it was good feeling free and not tense. We walked around while swinging my pillowcase singing our made-up song: 'my sack my sack my lovely lady sack', so mature I know! Finally, after so many phone calls she answered telling me I needed to get back to house. I didn't want to, it was like four so us girls planned a way to not go home, but not have to carry the case everywhere. So we told her where I was.

We even sang her our made-up song but unfortunately one of the girls made it worse by calling her a bitch. I quickly hung up hoping she hadn't heard it. After a while we saw her car pull up, the girls were hiding. I walked up, opened the door and threw my pillow in the car and ran. But they threw it out of the car and said if I didn't go home, she would ring the police. I rang Timmy my youth leader and told him what happened and how I didn't want to go home.

After a while I went to youth group, my carer knew where I was because I told her when It finished. She told me she didn't want to pick me up, I shrugged it off thinking she would get over her issue. As youth was coming to an end, I was sad. Youth was always a safe place for me which meant I sometimes felt safe and let my tears out. I talked to Tim and Jess for a bit, in the end Jess told me to follow her out another exit. Talking to Tim was a police officer, I was thankful that they saved me embarrassment, but I was beyond pissed at the carers. Tim and Jess hugged me, and I cried, upset about what had happened. I followed the cop to the police car and sat in the front. On the way home the cop and I made small talk, he asked me what had been happing and I told him. He told me how she rang him asking him to drag me out of youth group to embarrass me, and he told her not to tell him how to do his job. On the way home we drove past eldest sister's house and I told him how my sister lived on the street. When he dropped me home, he told me that if I get into an argument or don't feel safe to call him. It felt good to have someone who believed me, because everyone else, even eldest sister would always have turned it on me saying I should have been better, and it hurt because my carers would always act innocent and make me the bad guy. I know I also had done some things wrong and things I wasn't proud of.

The police officer talked with my carers and I went into my room. I had an urge to prove to everyone that I was not always to blame. Though what I was about to do was kind of illegal, I didn't care, at least I wasn't committing a big crime. I decided I was going to record them starting an argument. I knew they would because they always do. I walked into the kitchen, phone in hand and got out the ice cream and all hell broke loose. They were telling me I couldn't just get whatever I wanted (every other night they didn't care). We were arguing over anything and everything, at one put I just stopped talking and let them yell. Then she started pushing me lightly into my room, I told her I can walk into my room myself. Once I was in my room, she took my phone before I could even stop recording. After a while I decided I didn't want to stay any longer, so I told them I was leaving and going to the police station. I put my warm dressing gown on and my slippers and left. Of course, I wasn't going to walk all the way into town, Port Lincoln may be small but there are some weird people.

After Sunday nights problems, and with me leaving, I spent the week out near Cummins. It was about a 25 minute drive from Port Lincoln. I was on a farm, I'd been in this emergency care once before and loved it there. They had horses, which was a massive plus for me. It was a week getaway that I needed, I was always out patting the horses and had free time to be myself and get my mind into a good place. I was very hurt and broken, was I not good enough? What did I do to go through that many families, only to be left by myself with no family to go home to? Yes, I still had Mama and Daddo, but it wasn't the same. I didn't go to school for the week, foster kids don't have to go to school for the first week of them moving placements.

Thursday came and I had to pack my stuff on the way into town. I was informed that I was going back into the group home, the one I was in a couple years ago. I was happy to go there, unlike the first time. The first night was good, I was in the same room that I was in before. At first it was awkward with the other two girls, so I just kept to myself. There was also a worker that I didn't know but she was nice too. I later found out that there was only one worker that I knew from my first time in the home two years before. Luckily it was one of my favourite workers and she was also friends with my other favourite worker who doesn't work there anymore. I settled in pretty quickly and easily in the first week, I didn't unpack pretty much at all.

The first week was still hard though, because about three days after leaving my first placement since leaving Tumby, Mama and Daddo decided it was best to cut all contact. Reading those words broke me so much, all I could think of was that this was the end they didn't want anything to do with me. I cried so much, probably not as much as I did when I first moved, but it was still a lot of tears. I was surprised I survived the transition of moving without having Mama and Daddo's support and love, there was definitely challenges with this new no contact arrangement.

When I was upset and not in the best mindset, I did stupid things because I wasn't thinking straight. There were still times where I tried to message them hoping they would reply even though I knew they wouldn't. After a while I gave up, I had to step back and trust that God had it under control. If after a while they didn't want to be my parents, then I had to accept it, but I prayed that it wouldn't be the case and that they would still want to be my parents. I still had them on social media, but it hurt too much to see photos of them and wishing I was with them. I unfollowed them, so I didn't have keep hating myself for hurting them.

After a few weeks I started getting along with the other kids and the workers. I was closer friends with an amazing girl called Jade. Jade wasn't like my other friends unlike hung with the wrong crowds, she did drugs and stole things. Most people would take one glance and judge her and her friends. But I saw more to her then what she did, her actions didn't define her and I wanted to be the friend that she could turn back to when she needed someone. I also knew that there was a part of her that didn't want to do the stuff she did, and it was up to her to find that strength. One thing I admired about her was that she never forced me to do anything she knew I didn't want to – she knew my morals and respected me for that.

My God parents were moving away and I was sad. I was going to miss them, they were always there for me and I loved them so much. They never judged me and were always supportive, I was going to miss our Ben and Jerry dates and I knew with them moving I had no place to go to when I needed. But I knew I would be able to see them every now and then. Them leaving also meant I had to give the guitar back, so I was sad about that too. I made sure I played the guitar as much as I could before giving it back.

Band practice was good, it was something I could do through the week and was a safe place for me when I was upset. There was one person at music practice, 'Ana', she started being someone I could trust. She and her husband ran the band practice and they had a little daughter who was a little bit older than my baby sister and she was adorable. She always seemed to know when I was sad and was always there for me, ready to hug me when I needed a shoulder to cry on. Meeting her was one of the best things that had happened to me, she was there supporting me, telling me I was special and that I needed to stay alive and how much God loved me. She told me the truth, even when I didn't want to hear it.

One week I was in a bad place and was ready to end it all. I went to band practice and saw Ana, she knew something was wrong and that's something I sometimes didn't like about her. Normally I'm invisible, but she always knew when I was sad, I was looking at her feeling, lost and scared. I couldn't tell her but I hoped that that maybe she could see the fear in my eyes. She hugged me, 'What have you done?' she asked concern flooding her face. 'I haven't done anything, it's what I want to do,' I said with fear and brokenness. I regretted what I said as soon as it left my mouth, 'why do you want to die?' Ana asked quietly, as if everyone in the room could hear us. 'I can't do this, I can't, what's the point if I don't have a home?' I said thoughtful and heart broken. 'Don't say that, don't end your life, you are so special,' she said with tears fighting their way out of her eyes. 'I don't know anymore.e' I said as ters rolled down my face. 'Do you need a hug?' she asked. 'Yes.' After a few minutes we let go.

I was grateful for Ana, I always am, her hugs and being around her made my problems disappear for a bit. There were days I wished it were Mama, but I knew Mama was happier without me (or so I thought).

Christmas was coming up faster than I wanted, eldest sister and Nikki's partner had a joint birthday that I went to. There were so many people, I even saw a couple who lived next door to mum growing up, they were an older couple. It was good catching up with them, big sister didn't come, she was officially not part of the family.

Even though she had hurt me so much I still cared about her, but eldest sister and Dad didn't want me to have anything to do with her and I knew if I did then they would disown me. So I was stuck, and it was so tiring and hard, I wanted a break from everyone. Big sister was also due any day and I knew there was going to be a chance that I was going to miss the birth of my niece or nephew.

Eldest sister and Nikki's partner have been together for a long time; with two beautiful girls that I love with all my heart, and another baby on the way. We have all been waiting for them to get married, so it was an exciting moment went he went on his knee and proposed to eldest sister. I was beyond excited and her ring was beautiful. I was happy for them, yes they had issues and arguments as everyone does, but they were good parents.

I wasn't one for having a boyfriend at my age, I'd much rather wait until I was older. I have had a few boyfriends, some weren't good and hurt me, and some didn't last long enough to be classified as a boyfriend. I guess I had gotten hurt by family again and again and after that boyfriends couldn't hurt me when we broke up. And growing closer to God and being the best Christian I could be, I knew I wanted a Christian guy who would make me want to grow closer to God.

Soon enough it was super close to Christmas. I loved Christmas growing up, and yes I would still see eldest sister and the kids for Christmas, but I knew I was still alone and I wanted to have a family and be in a home for Christmas, not a homeless shelter. Luckily, I had incredible people in my life who didn't want me spending it alone, so my day was busy. In the morning I had breakfast with eldest sister and the family, Mum came, and we weren't happy. I loved my Meum, but I am a follower, so I listened to people and let them control me/ I don't know why I hadn't learned to not let people do that, considering I had been through a lot of pain and trauma because of it. After breakfast I went back home for lunch, we had a big lunch and I made chocolate mousse and we jammed to music that wasn't even Christmas music.

Jade and I had our favourite worker on and it was a good afternoon. For dinner I went out with Timmy and Jess and their family to a beach, I was truly grateful for them treating me as their family. I had a great night with them, they got me presents which weren't necessary. They got me a dress and a reindeer teddy called Candy Cane which I loved. While at the beach we saw a guy way too drunk in the water and dancing, at one stage he stripped naked, and at that point we knew it was time to get out of there.

That night I laid in my bed staring at the roof while tears rolled down my face. It had been a good day, yes, but my heart longed to be home. I couldn't help but think that they probably had had an amazing day as a family with no thought of me. I mean why would they? I fucked up really bad. 'I'm sorry I didn't mean to!' I cried out to God. The past few weeks had been a mess, leaving home had broken me. Moving from other foster homes hadn't made me cry us much as leaving this home did. I had known from the start that leaving was going to hurt like a bitch. Did I blame them for breaking promises? Not at all!

I did get a message from Mama a few days before Christmas, asking if I wanted to see them after Christmas. They were coming down with Kayla my cousin, I was so excited but I knew that the start of contact again meant rules. Even though I was happy that I could start seeing and talking to them, I was worried that the wait wouldn't be worth it. What if it was all different? What if we started seeing each other and they decide it's too hard? I didn't want to mess it up, so I wrote a list of rules for myself of what I could and couldn't do. It was a strict list, but I knew it would prevent them from giving up. I also feared that they wouldn't see me as their daughter anymore, and not only that, but I also worried what others thought of me. I was disappointed in what I had done but I didn't want others to judge me for what I did. I also wouldn't be surprised if God hadn't forgiven me, so I regularly said sorry to God.

The first time I saw them since the no contact message wasn't as bad as I thought. We had a great time and my baby sister was so excited to see me. Mama and Daddo went to an appointment, so I got some time with my favourite big cousin. As always, we hung out and acted stupid; but the time went too quick and soon it was time to go. I said goodbye holding, back the tears. It was harder to hold them back when my baby sister realised that I wasn't going with them and she started crying. I knew it would be hard on her because she wouldn't know what was going on it, must be horrible having your big sissy with you one day and gone the next, especially at her age!

After our first catchup I was still messaging them, mainly Mama, and it was good being able to talk to them again. We just talked about our days but I made sure I kept in mind the rules that I had come up with. These rules included things like; not messaging all the time unless they do first; not to talk about my problems, especially about mental health because that was one of the reasons I had to leave; when in a new home, try to build trust with them and go to them about issues before Mama and Daddo. Some other rules were that after a few months I could start letting them in. I made these rules because I couldn't lose them, they were the only family who loved me for me and were there for me.

I never really knew the reasons why I had to leave, but I knew it might have to do with my mental health. I knew it was hard for them, being young and only just starting their own family, then they brought me in while they were trying to jungle owning half the doctor's clinic. So I had never, and I could never, blame them for making the tough decision. I had a lot of problems that I had bottled up and it was hard, not only on them, but on me. I did envy them though; I would do anything to have a break from myself. My problems tired me out too. They said they would always be my family and nothing would stop that, and I wanted to trust them, I really did, but it was just too hard. But even if I wanted to, I couldn't hate them! It's not their fault, I guess it was mine. It's something I would have to live with, it might kill me or break me, but that's if the system didn't break me first.

The new year rolled in and I had no idea what 2019 would bring. Saying I scared would be an understatement. It's a new school year, too, and being in year ten meant I only had three years of school left. It also meant I had three years until I was 18, so I could get out of the system. I had lots of fears for the new year: what if I failed in school? What if Mama and Daddo didn't want me anymore? What if I had to do all this police and court stuff alone? I couldn't do it without Mama and Daddo.

But I had to focus on the now, I was always worrying about the future so I kind of had to trust God with this. We had new people come to the group home, with new rooms because Jade decided to leave me there alone. But I didn't want to make friends in the house, so I didn't talk to them. Jade and I had great fun and because of her my time in this house was not as bad. Being in the house did teach me a lot like: marijuana smells so bloody bad, and so do bongs and they look gross too. I was grateful to Jade letting me hang around when she smoked bongs, living in the house full of people doing drugs, because I learnt that drugs are gross, and I would never do them. But we did fun stuff, some probably weren't the right thing to do, but oh well, you only lived once. Hanging with Jade was lots of fun, she was the biggest bitch but I loved her. Being around Jade, I let my rebel side go wild. We were the shitheads of the house, ask the workers they would agree!

At one stage there was this kid who was younger than us and shy. He got into a lot of trouble with the law, so we acted like his big sisters. I felt sorry for him because he felt unheard, and I knew that there was a reason he had done what he did. It was proof the system breaks you and turns you into what society calls a bad person. We always covered up for him (well mainly Jade), like one day he set off all the fire extinguishers so I laughed and cleaned up before the worker came out. But the worker would've seen it anyway because the house had cameras everywhere. Then he put sticks in all the locks, which was annoying because we had a locked cupboard with food so we couldn't get to it. That day was pretty busy and by the end of it the police, came so Jade played some rap music while we watched them arrest him.

But now she had left, and I went back to being a good kid… who was I kidding? I wasn't who I use to be, I was ashamed of who I had become. I had lost friends, Georgia and I had an argument and I felt bad but people change. Life had impacted me in a different way, and I knew that if I wanted to change my behaviour I could. One thing I wouldn't miss about Jade is having her bang down my door to wake me up in the morning because she had somewhere to be and couldn't get dropped off unless I went. Luckily for me, I'm easily bribed with food so she bought me a feed!

My fight with Georgia wasn't actually something that bad, it was just hard for me to come to terms with the fact that my best friend could still go to my family's home and spend time with them and I couldn't. It hurt that I couldn't be there to see the new things my baby sister had learned. I took it out on Georgia, and I felt bad because it was my fault, but when I was upset I took it out on either those I cared about or myself. So we got into an argument because I was upset that she got to see them, and I was still, in a sense, grieving the fact that I had left so I wasn't in the right headspace. She took offence and didn't talk to me even though I said I was sorry. I hadn't wanted to hurt her, but I couldn't not tell her that telling me everything that's going on with them wasn't okay. I wasn't going to tell her to stop seeing them, that would be unfair, but I just wanted her to stop telling me about them until I was ready. I also got into an argument with Lucy becasue she wasn't happy about me hanging with Jade. She thought I was changing, which pissed me off – everything pissed me off. I was on short fuse after leaving home and it sucked.

But what made everything a bit better was a phone call from Ardy. It was good having them still see me as their granddaughter, even when I didn't live at home. I felt so loved and special knowing that I had grandparents who loved me; a grandparent's love is something so special, maybe even more than a parent's love. I never had a real family, and now I have one and I hope and pray it stays that way. They were understanding considering they saw Mama as their own daughter (even if she isn't on paper). That's what I loved about this family, they didn't care about DNA, just about calling each other family and loving each other no matter what.

Ardy and Lizzy were the main family who talked to me, which was very nice, but I still was fearful. So I kept my distance and didn't tell them much about my problems. Ana was one of the main people I talked to, but even then I felt like a burden. I felt safe and comfortable around her, so I would blurt out what's wrong and I regret it straight away – I couldn't have her leave my life. But I knew that God put people in our lives, and we couldn't control who leaves and stays, but I hoped and prayed to God that he wouldn't put me through unnecessary pain, unless he had a good plan. Luckily for me I still had Mama and Daddo in my life, and even though I was scared it wouldn't last long, I still tried to enjoy it and not have any worries.

Luckily, I still had a few weeks before school started and I decided (actually I was forced) to compete in 'Teen Tunarama'. Tunarama was an event that happened where I lived in January every year. To win we had to help at events and raise money, I was in the competition with 4 other girls, one of them was a close friend of mine, but I also knew the other three. The other girls sometimes complained, but I just enjoyed myself and knew that even if I didn't want to be part of this I might as well win!

The days before the competition were good, we did a bake sale to raise money and went from store to store to pick up prizes. When the weekend came of the event we had to help with mini competitions for kids, some of these were the: prawn toss, salmon toss (both were fake) and sandcastle comps. We also had to go on stage in front of the whole town! I brought two dresses from an op shop, they were really pretty. I got heels and we got someone to come and do my makeup. Mama, Daddo and my baby sister came as well for the first night. I was happy I had them there and I got in some sissy time! I even wrote Georgia a sorry note, I wished she was there too. It was the end of the weekend – after the fireworks and rides – the last night and we sang and danced on the dance floor with a group of girls competing in Miss Tunarama. I even got a photo with two guys who were really good singers, and kinda cute (not gonna lie hehe).

And finally, the moment came, it was time to find out who the winner was! Mama and Daddo weren't there, but eldest sister was so that was good. I still didn't have contact with big sister, so she wasn't there, so many people were in the crowd and it was nerveraking being on stage. I was so sure they weren't going to call my name, as they said the third, then the second and finally they said "and the winner" I just wanted it to be over, it felt like forever at first I thought I was hearing things then my mind finally registered "is Felicity" I couldn't believe I was so shocked but happy.

Mama made new promises, things like: I would always be their daughter, or they wouldn't leave my life, that they would always love me. I wanted to trust her, but it still hurts like hell, and even though I couldn't fully admit it because I blamed myself, I knew I had to protect myself so I didn't get hurt again. I could never blame them – they didn't mean to hurt me – they were just trying to protect themselves and their family. I know they loved me so much and it killed them to let me go. But I hurt them a lot, so I needed to protect them from me too.

Baby B's birthday came and went but I didn't get to celebrate. I was sad I didn't ,but the following week Ardy and Lizzy came over so we all went out for lunch for a late birthday (and an early one for me). Even though in a perfect world I would've loved to be there on the day, I also was truly grateful that I still had a family, even if it was broken, it was perfect in my eyes and I loved every bit of it. We had lunch and gave presents. Ardy and Lizzy went on a cruise, so they got me gifts, a bracelet and cap. I also took Baby B for a walk on the beach for quality Sissy time, which I lapped up, before they left.

I found that even after seeing the fam it still took a while for me to realise that this was my new life and it wouldn't ever be the same. I learned that I would be sadder before I was finally on a high, and I knew it would take time to learn how to be a family again and how to trust and love again. My birthday was also in a few weeks, so I took time to look forward to that and plan my big, Sweet 16. I wanted a big party, I always had pool parties with a few friends, but I always seen Sweet 16 parties and how big they were, so I wanted the same. Obviously, that was unrealistic considering I didn't have many friends, so I didn't know how to make it special.

Band was good, we had a worship workshop where we had a couple come with their kids and we spent a whole day with them telling us the power of free worship where we sang whatever was in our hearts. He also taught us about prophetic words, how we could listen to God and what he wanted us to tell others. He taught us about how we needed to lay down everything for God, our whole life, because he sent his son to die for us and Jesus gave up everything for us.

Other things that stood out was how we shouldn't focus on others but on him, and our past isn't an issue because he loved us no matter our past, our sins and our choices. Another thing that I knew I struggled with was how we are judged by what we say, and we are called to be faithful and if we don't think or act like Jesus did then he had died in vain. Personally, I didn't really step out of my comfort zone to talk about God.

And finally, he talked about how spiritual worship and song is. Worship draws people in, and how when we are led by the spirit it doesn't become about us but him. I really liked how he spoke, telling us how it wasn't about music but stepping out in faith.

I was glad I had things like band and my party to look forward to. It was a good and much-needed distraction. A week and a bit after the workshop it was my birthday and all the planning for was worth it.

Like many things in my life, I had found a way to ruin a surprise that Mama was planning for me I couldn't help but read the message I guess curiosity did kill the cat. I felt horrible that night and it was worse because my boyfriend and I got into an argument and broke up, though in a way I wasn't upset because I was used to it. So instead of getting rid of the idea, Mama and I decided to plan my birthday together. I liked planning my birthday with my Mama because it was special. Mama mainly took care of invitations while I planned decorations. Then DCP threatened to cancel my party for some stupid reason, luckily they didn't, and the party went on. The morning of my birthday my worker who makes amazing sausage rolls, played music for me. One song was Birthday Bitch which became my favourite song.

For my party there was a photo wall set up; a lolly stall; photobooth; and I had a few friends, family and family friends over. I even had Georgia over for my birthday, she had forgiven me and we were friends again. We weren't as close as we use to be which was sad, but I prayed that we would be that close again one day. I had Daddo and Mama, but the only biological family I had was eldest sister. Big sister and I kept in contact, so she messaged me. I didn't tell anyone that I was in contact with big sister because I was afraid that they would disown like they had big sister, but I also knew big sister had no family. Dad didn't come to my party or buy me anything, which was no surprise, but I didn't let that ruin a good day with my real family.

My birthday didn't finish there! Luckily, our family believe in birthday weeks, because the following weekend Grandma (Mama's mum) came down and had lunch with me. I was truly blessed to still have a family who loved me and had not given up on me no matter what! It was hard getting used to the fact that they wouldn't leave, and I knew it would take time. But it was another birthday with them, so another milestone.

After my birthday it was pretty chilled. I went to school and avoided most people, sometimes I did my work. I had one teacher who I swore had something against me, like he would always get angry at me and he never understood why I didn't do work or didn't want to participate in work and groups. School had always been a trigger for my bad mental health and anxiety, people always told me it was a good distraction, but It wasn't. I struggled more when I went to school and this teacher didn't help. But my English teacher was amazing, he was supportive and fun. I did really well in English which was no surprise. And then there was math and science, another subject that I struggled in because I had an Indian teacher. He was nice and tried to be supportive, but I didn't understand what he said or his way of teaching.

So, when I got really overwhelmed, instead of going home because I knew they wouldn't let me, I would skip school. It wasn't every day, and rarely it would be weekly. One day I went out and went to the beach, I chilled there and went for a big walk. It was an adventure and it was great. I texted both Ana and Mama, they both asked why I skipped so I told them what had been happening. It went from me skipping to an MPR (missing person's report), something that the workers had to do when I didn't come home at curfew, which was 9:30 and 10:00 pm on weekends. Just like school, I only went on an MPR when I was overwhelmed, and I didn't really talk to the workers when I felt unsafe so instead of self-harming, I stayed out at night to keep myself safe.

Every time I stayed out and got picked up by the cops, which would be well after 12 am, I would hide. The police weren't really looking anyway, they always drove past when I was in obvious places. But I would get tired and let them find me, every time they picked me up, they were always nice and gave me advice. When I went on MPR I stayed home from school and slept.

I had good things going on though, even if I was struggling too much to focus on the positives. Being 16 meant that I could start the process of independent living which is where I would get to have my own house. As excited as I was, I also knew that it was going to be a lot of work and stressful, but I was ready. I could never be in a family; I had messed that up time and time again. I didn't think I was family material anymore, I guess I grew too independent. I had had to learn to look after myself which meant that when I was in a family I didn't know how to take a step back and be looked after, even though I was a KID. As I have learned this year, having people care made it way too overwhelming for me and I lashed out or shut down. So independent living was a better option.

I was surprised that Georgia and Lucy stuck with being my friends. Lucy and I had our ups and downs, though I went to her house and we drunk alcohol – all was well. I didn't really tell her much about my problems because she had a history of being mean and telling me to get over it, or that I always complained about my problems;

but she told me about her problems which I happily listened to and supported her with. I had noticed that she also didn't like it when I gave her advice, I tried so hard to be a good friend and there were times when I felt like I wasn't appreciated by her or any of the friends I'd had. Over time I had to learn to ignore that feeling and move on. One particular day, Lucy came for advice and I told her what I thought of the situation and she got angry at me. I wanted to sort it out, so we met at a park and she threated to punch me, but she wasn't someone who could fight because she hadn't ever had a physical fight.

Trying to help her while keeping my mental health in check was draining. I couldn't say that to her though because she would feel bad and wouldn't have anyone to go to. At least I had people like Ash and Ana who I could turn to, but even then I felt bad for burdening them with my problems. There was only so much I could do to help her, and I knew it was up to her to take control of her life. I even encouraged her to talk to her counsellor but she didn't want to. She told me I wasn't helping and that she didn't want to talk to me for a while. I was used to that. We have had many arguments which had led to us not talking. That wasn't what affected me, it was the fact I used all my energy helping her and it felt like it was thrown in my face. I knew she was struggling, so I didn't get angry and I gave her time, but in that time I was falling and breaking, I felt like I was drowning but no one notice. That's what they say about drowning, it's a silent killer and it is the same for depression too.

I kind of know why she acted the way she did, because there are times when I had gone to people for help and I gotten defensive. But after a few weeks, sometimes months, I would look back and realise that there was something behind what they had said. I was getting drained, losing my strength to fight, and I was ready to give up.

I was so drained that I had planned to kill myself. I couldn't do it anymore, I was called names by one of the girls in the house, which I ignored but I didn't have friends at school or in general. I didn't have family, Mama and Daddo were still my 'parents', or so they promised, but I didn't know how long that would last. So, at the end of the week I decided that I would kill myself. I didn't say anything to anyone, one reason was that I didn't have anyone, even though I got along with workers and sometimes told them about my problems.

I went to the park which was across the road and sat there looking at the stars. I noted how pretty they were and how much I wished I was up there. I messaged Lucy, who still wasn't wanting anything to do with me and I told her 'whatever happens, don't blame yourself, you didn't know what was going to happen,' and some other things. She took it the wrong way and started getting angry and defensive. I didn't know how to tell her what I meant without saying I had planned to die. With tears rolling down chasing each other I cried out to God 'why have you left me? Where are you?' my voice breaking. 'I am giving myself three days to live, so if you really wanted me to live on this earth then give me a good reason,' I said, a demand and a promise seeped through my words.

I didn't stay out that night, I went straight into my room. Some nights I would stay up late and chat with the workers, but not tonight. I went straight to my room and cried myself to sleep. The next day I went to school, trying to act as normal as possible. It was Thursday which meant band practice and because I didn't have a guitar, most weeks I would go on multimedia to do church slides. Sometimes I did practice guitar, but I was not good enough for church, which was okay. Sometimes I struggled with the slides, especially when I learned new songs, but I had gotten the hang of it.

By the end of Thursday I had English and I was quiet in class, which was normal but I stayed back and talked to my teacher. He was amazing guy and we talked. Somehow we got onto the topic of mental health and I broke down in tears. I told him I couldn't do it anymore – I wasn't strong enough. I told him that I had given myself three days to live. He looked like he was about to cry, I knew he cared a lot and I felt bad but I couldn't back out. He told me that he wasn't working and he wouldn't see me until Monday so I couldn't die. But I whispered 'I'm sorry I... I can't,' and left.

I wasn't thinking about going to band, but maybe being around Christians might give me a reason to live. So, I had gotten dropped off at church and sat with my friends. That night we talked about prophetic words and we did an activity where we had a name picked out and wrote what we felt that God had put in our hearts.

While we had worship in the background, I went to the back of the church and sat down. I couldn't hold back the tears and I cried out to God, my tears were silent prayers. It was times like this that I wished I was home being held by Mama, but I wasn't. I didn't know where to go from here I was scared, but I also wasn't. I had a few friends come up and see if I was okay, then I started having a panic attack and I was crying so much that I couldn't see clearly. Ana came up and hugged me, and every now and then my friends would come up and give me a hug. I couldn't tell them why I was crying, but it was killing me holding it in. I didn't want to die I just wanted the pain and sadness to end. Even self-harming wasn't giving me release from the pain.

I was getting ready to go and had gone to get my stuff. Ash came up and gave me a hug, I ended up crying even more and I told her everything. She had always been someone I could trust and I looked up to the amount of times she has just been there.

She was there when I found out from Mama that they felt they couldn't keep me safe so I couldn't live at home. Ash was an important person in my life, and I couldn't thank her enough, but I knew that what I told her would make her sad. We talked and she prayed for me, it meant a lot and I also told her about the issues I had with Lucy and how it was affecting me.

She had me for the activity and gave me the note she wrote, though I didn't agree with bits of it. Stuff like how she wrote that my name means happiness and my joy. She said it would shine and be my strength, I was unsure what joy she saw in me, but she wrote a verse from the book of Psalm in verse 41 'the lord delivers them in times of trouble, the lord protects and preserves them' and another verse, 'there may be pain in the night but joy comes in the morning' which I knew I needed to read.

I don't know why but talking to her helped a little bit, she prayed for me as she did I felt at peace, that the chains had broken off. I wasn't sure how long this might last but I wanted to hold onto the feeling for now. I had learned that while I wasn't struggling with my depression and anxiety, I could take time to grow stronger, learn some skills to help me when I would fall back into the depression. I was worried it was not going to get better.

I wouldn't say that I had gotten better after that night going at band practice, I wasn't happy or sad so I guess I was numb. I didn't tell Mama or Daddo that I thought of dying, I felt that if I did then that could be a set back and I couldn't risk losing them. I was having a few issues with my biological family and if I lost Mama and Daddo I was afraid I wouldn't have any family, so I had to be careful. I don't know why my family were like this, I loved them so much but they hurt me. I felt like I never could win, I felt like I was always at fault and any wrong move would make them cut me out. I stuck around because I was too afraid of them talking badly about me. I talked to big sister, but I kept it a secret and eldest sister had another baby, so I was an aunty to 4 nieces now (including big sister's baby). I had always felt like they blamed everything on me, it sucked because I had tried being a good sister and daughter but I felt like I wasn't doing enough… like I wasn't enough. It sucked that when I needed them the most, they weren't there. I didn't even have much contact with Mum, I had cut her out fully, and I only talked to Dad a bit, but it was hard.

He changed a lot when he first came into my life. It was good that he accepted Mama and Daddo and didn't have a problem with them, but once I left home he changed. He told me how they weren't my parents anymore and it felt like I was always arguing with him. This wasn't how I had ever pictured a family, but it was what I had grown up with. This broken family with an absent Dad, a mum who neglected her children, an older sister who was a parent to us until she left and lived with our Dad, and another older sister who hurt me growing up and now I was unsure if she was a better sister.

Yes, she hurt me, but there were times when she was a good sister. Times where she cared for and loved me. She would stay up, checking on me when we were kids at night and making sure I was okay. My foster parents would tell her it was okay, and that they were looking after me.

I didn't even know what family was anymore, I had seen many different families and I wanted one who would love me. I know I had Mama and Daddo, but if I had to choose who would I choose? Probably Mama and Daddo not because I don't love my other family, I do, but Mama and Daddo are good parents. They cheer me on and stick by my side, they loved me for me and wouldn't give up (at least I hoped they wouldn't), but I'm trying to trust God. I had Easter Camp coming up soon and I asked Mama if they could come to the family night because it was kind of our thing. It would be two years since I had met them and I wanted to see them. She said maybe, so I was hoping they would come up. Like every year we had a dress up, and the theme was under the sea and over the sea, so I decided I wanted to get creative.

I had gotten a big box and cut out two sides into a whale shape, I put two holes on both sides so that I could be in the middle of the whale and walk around with the string on my shoulders. To add some more fun, I painted it and drew Jonah praying in the whale like the bible story. Georgia was coming on camp and she was getting dropped off by Mama. Lucy wasn't coming, we were still in an argument that sucked, but it was a good time to have a break. I went to the site with my youth group and one of our leaders was taking us. On the way we sang to random songs, it's always fun driving with them we always sing and have fun.

During camp the speaker spoke in depth about a book in the bible called Colossians. He told us how Jesus is bigger than our problems and how he is powerful. He told us how Jesus was the first to be reborn from the dead, and how we lived in a world where we were always under pressure by others, but through God we are filled; we were no longer pressured by earthly things because we have died and been reborn again through God.

He told us to ask ourselves how big is our Jesus? Was our problems and suffering bigger than him? This set me back and it made me think: *Was I letting my problems be bigger and blind me from God's truth?* He gave us a lot of good points and something else that really stood out was when he told us 'just as a bear can ride a bike, Christians can sin, but its unfitting.' As Christians we are something different than what we were before, so we should stand out.

Our life as Christians is no longer on earth, but with God and following him so we shouldn't live like the rest of the world, we should put to death the earthly things. Christianity is not about what we don't do but about what we do. It's easier to see faults than to see the good. The weekend was good and when Georgia got dropped off, I saw Mama and they gave me some Easter eggs, I guess I was still a part of the family.

They did end up coming to the family night and I was so happy to see Baby B. After doing plays for the parents each group had a task to do, either something to read or a prayer. My group did a bible reading and we made it into a play. I read the bible verse and once we were done and walking back to our seats Baby B came running to my arms. It was cute, I loved when she called me Sissy and hugged me. It made my life worth it. After dinner I went outside and sat down. Mama came and sat next to me, and her arms wrapped around me as we looked up at the stars.

We talked, I cried and she held me just like when I was home. It still hurt, I don't know when it would ever stop but what I did know was that we could choose our own family and I didn't know what made a family but being around Mama and Daddo, I know I feel safe, loved, wanted and accepted. Even though it hurt and I didn't know how long it would last, I would fight to stay their daughter.

Even if it didn't work at least I would know what it was like to have a family.

After camp, feeling happy that I won best dressed, I didn't want to go home. But throughout the weeks after camp the thought *how big is my Jesus* swam around my mind. Despit this my demons didn't care about how big my Jesus was. They cared about pulling me into the darkness. I tried swimming to the surface. I didn't try to make friends at school, I was nice to everyone and had fun, but I wasn't friends with them as such. People tried being my friend and I appreciated it, but I didn't want to have friends and have to open up about my life. Some teachers were really supportive as well, which was good, but I also had teachers that annoyed me, so I refused to listen in their class. Some days I couldn't pay attention – my mind was way too busy. I didn't feel like anywhere was my safe place; school sucked, home sucked, I had church, dance and youth which was my family.

Being in the home was pretty bad, the workers were funny and nice but I didn't feel too supported. And the other kids weren't as good. But I was still close with one of the girls who was there when I first moved in. She was like Jade in many ways and was fun to be around. We once had a food fight, it was raining, and we went outside with flour and got a handful and threw it at each other.

I also got along with the other guy in the house even though he ate us out of house and home. He was a nice person but I did bully him a bit or as I called it – taught him resilience. One of the girls took her hurt out on me, I was older than her but she wasn't very nice. She called me many names but the workers didn't do anything.

One night we were home alone which was normal because the workers went home between 7 pm and 9 pm. I was watching Tv and she changed the channel. So here we were fighting over the Tv, so I turned it off and she was calling me names and said 'no wonder your parents didn't want you.' Those words were like knives, I could take a lot of insults but insults like that affect me especially as she was in the same situation as me. After that I couldn't hold myself back and I said something, not as bad as her comment, but something I knew wasn't nice.

She didn't like what I said and started kicking me. I was stunned and the kicks hurt a bit. I knew I had to control my emotions so I went into my room. She rung the worker who came back and talked to her, and then I walked out. I didn't want to go back there. A little while later the police came, and I told them everything but had to go home. I locked myself in my room and rung Georgia, I didn't have anyone else to ring. The next morning, I was told I was kicked out but had to have a meeting in four days to see if I could come back. I was shocked that they had kicked me out because I was apparently 'verbally abusive to her', but I packed anyway. We had cameras in the house so they saw the footage of her kicking me and she got kicked out too.

I stayed in emergency care for days and there was talk about moving to Adelaide because there wasn't anywhere here for me to live. But I didn't tell many people because every time they'd said that I ended up staying. Monday came and the meeting happened, it didn't go well at all. I told them I didn't want to stay in a place where I don't feel supported. So they said that was fine.

When I went back to the DCP office they had to make phone calls so I made some calls too. I rang Ash and told her and cried. I also rang Ardy Pa and told him. He was the only one I wanted to talk to. Mama and Daddo were in America, I did briefly message, but I didn't want to say too much.

Later I was told I was going to Adelaide and was going into emergency care until the end of the week, where I would be moving into a group home with other girls. It was around the Adelaide Hills which was where I wanted to live after school.

I wasn't sure what was going to happen, I cried out to God *what is going to happen, please don't leave me*? I was going to miss my church, miss seeing Mama and Daddo once a month but there was something inside me telling me to *trust God it's going to be okay*. I realised that this was something that would put me out of my comfort zone and I knew somehow God was going to use me so much and I would be able to fulfil whatever he planned, even if I would have ups and downs I had to trust him.

The flight to Adelaide was smooth, I don't like planes but I was caught up thinking about what was next in my life. I wasn't worried about moving to a new place, I didn't have anything to lose only to gain and I knew God had it under control. It was late by the time we got into the city, which was a 45-minute flight. We had to wait a while for a lady to pick us up to take me to my new placement that I would stay at until the end of the week. Then I would get to go to my long-term placement. Once we got picked up, I got Hungry Jacks and was dropped off; we had to wait ages because the worker and little girl I had to stay with weren't home and we didn't have a spare key.

But we got the spare key and went inside and the room I was staying in was like a hotel room with a big window. My bed was a double-sized bed and it was amazing. I set everything down and went down the small stairs. After a while my social worker left and hugged me, making sure I was okay. I bit my lip to hold back the tears as we said goodbye and even though she can annoy the hell out of me, sometimes she didn't support me or think about what I thought and felt I needed, I was going to miss her.

But she did have her days where I saw that somewhere in her heart she tried and cared, even if she was slow to do so. That night I met the worker and the little girl, who was way too young to ever have to be in a residential house instead of with a family, who was cute. I felt for her, if it was hard for me to not have a family and I couldn't even comprehend how difficult it was for her.

I didn't know her story, but I knew if it didn't affect her now it would as she grew up. It affects all us kids in care, unless you are lucky enough to have a good family who loved you but even then you have the trauma. I went to my room and rang Ardy Pa to let him know that I had landed safe and talked to him for a bit. But because I had already told him everything earlier that day, I didn't have to say anything else. I then rang my Grandma and Gran and told them both what had happened and what the week looked like. I was happy I actually caught Gran because she worked as a nurse and so she worked crazy hours.

After chats with my favourite sets of grandparents I thought I would ring Hayley one of my biggest supports I wanted her in the loop as she has been there for my sisters and I since a young age, but she didn't reply. She then messaged me asking if I was out in town after curfew again, considering it was like 10:30. I said 'nah I don't think I want to walk around in the big city this late,' because unlike my home town which is a 'city' (but seems more like a town) this city is well… BIG. Then I told her what had happen and everything leading up to now. After a big day and lots of tears I went to sleep, which was full of me being restless.

The next morning, I slept and chilled in bed before getting ready for the day and meeting new workers. I also had to get a script for my medication because I didn't have it with me. Some of the workers were really nice and I had good conversations with some. I was shy around new people and didn't really talk. I never really processed moving properly I hadn't thought, but I also didn't mind because I felt it was something God had in store for me.

I also went and caught up with big sister which I was happy about because I hadn't seen her for maybe a year, and I hadn't met my baby niece. We went to a mall and walked around, and I got extra cuddles and kisses with my baby niece. I loved being an aunty and I was going to miss my nieces back home, especially bubs who was born not long ago, but I knew moving meant time with a niece who I hadn't met or seen at all for her first months of life. Once I got home from the mall, I had some down time and read my bible, and that night we watched the Voice on TV.

Daddo, Mama and Baby B were in America visiting my aunty, so I didn't tell them much about why I had moved because I didn't want them worrying. Although I didn't think they would because I felt they were happier without me.

Near the end of the week I went out for lunch with two ladies; one was a placement coordinator and one was a placement manager. They were really nice and funny, I got along with them and I hoped that this new start would be the change I needed. I couldn't afford to move again unless I was moving into my own house through independent living.

I also had a phone call from my counsellor, which I appreciated so much. She had always been there for me and was someone I trusted a lot. I was glad I had her there rejoicing in my highs and achievements, but also helping me in my lows and failures. She never judged me and I am thankful for that.

Friday was the day I would move into my new home and I was excited but nervous. There was only one girl, the other two apparently didn't come home much, so I was glad I wouldn't be to too overwhelmed. I packed the night before and said goodbye to the little girl because I wouldn't see her in the morning as she would go to school and I would sleep in. The drive to my new home was quick and it was a scenic drive, I was happy that I was going to live in a beautiful area.

Gran wanted to catch up but I couldn't because today was my moving-in day. I was sad I hadn't seen her in what felt like forever but it wasn't that long because I saw her when I saw Mama for Mother's Day and for Daddo's birthday before they left.

Once I got to my new home, I was in awe. There was a servo down the road and scrub around the house. Even the inside of the house was beautiful, it was modern and big – nothing like the group and residential homes I had lived in before. I met the other girl briefly but she went into her room. It reminded me of myself whenever new people moved in after Jade had left.

It was definitely different to what I was used to, but I loved it. I met a couple of the workers and they were really nice. I didn't know what would be next in my life, what the next weeks and months would bring. I was scared but excited, kind of like the bible verse in the end of proverbs 30:25 'she is clothed with strength and dignity and laughs without fear of the future.'

The first week in my new home was surprisingly really good, I stayed in a small room they called the 'Harry Potter' room. I didn't watch Harry Potter so I didn't have a clue what it meant. I hadn't started school because my social worker, like many times before, was slow getting it done. I also couldn't help myself compare this home to my old home, this one felt more like a home than the other house and this one was bigger. We had Netflix and an axolotl, who didn't have a name because each time new kids came, he got a new name. But the workers weren't any better or worse than my old ones, they were just as nice and caring, but these ones probably showed they cared more.

The other girl and I talked a bit and got along, which was good. She stayed at the back of the house in the unit, which was the same as the hut at the back of the home I was in. The unit was much bigger and it had two rooms of a fairly decent size, dining and kitchen and a decent lounge room as well. The bathroom also had a washing machine.

It was homely, just like the big house, and I knew I was home and hopefully I wouldn't have to move again. I didn't think I could handle moving until I turned 18. I was going back home very soon which I was excited about because I got to see my family and church friends/family. When I went home it was my first time flying alone which was nerve-racking but it wasn't as bad as I thought.

I was staying with a friend for a few nights which was good, we had a great time and I also saw Lucy, but it wasn't the same and I knew we had drifted apart. It was hard spending a lot of time with her. I also saw Jade which was good. I then went to eldest sister and got to see all my nieces, they were happy to see me and I had missed them so much so it was good having some aunty time. I loved being an aunty but I loved being a big sissy more, it was more special having a baby sister to look up to me. I couldn't wait for Daddo and Mama to have another baby that I could love, teach and watch grow.

I got to see them which was a blessing, and Baby B was happy to see me. She had grown so much, and I had missed them a lot, it was good spending time with them. Going to church was a highlight, everyone was happy and surprised to see me and it was good to be home. That church had been my safe place and my rock, the people in church were like family.

A couple of days before I had to go home I went out for lunch with Ana and her little daughter. I had missed her a lot, she was always there for me and I hoped it would always stay that way despite the move. I was excited to go to my new home, but it made me sad that I no longer considered this place home.

My time visiting had come to an end and it was time to go home. I was not complaining, the flight home was not bumpy but I was still anxious about what could happen. Once home I unpacked and the days went as per usual. Some days it was just me and the workers because the other girl – New house friend – went to school, but this meant I had gotten to know the workers a bit more. They all seemed cool, lucky for me one was even a Christian and this made me feel more comfortable.

I spent some weekends with Ardy Pa and Nan at their house and I found that it had been a good getaway and something that I should've had back when I was at the other house. Sometimes I even got to stay at their block on the river, the first time I was there I was uneasy because it was a new place. We stayed in our own caravan and I didn't sleep. But it was beautiful and I took the time to connect with God to have a break, recharge.

Gran and Pa (Daddo's mum and dad) also came for an afternoon and went for a canoe and ride in the boat. I didn't know where I would be without them, they had stuck with me, all of the grandparents had never left my side. Even though I hurt Mama and Daddo a lot they didn't see me how I saw me, and that was what I loved about them. They forgave me and didn't see me as any less now than they did then. Same with Daddo and Mama, I am was so lucky to have them and to call them family. I don't know where I would be without them all.

As the weeks went on Mama and Daddo let me Facetime them once a month. I was happy we were moving forward, it was hard having all these rules: cans and cannot about us being a family, but I knew I had to follow the rules and not overstep any boundaries because I couldn't lose them. They were the only family who really believed in me and loved me, who didn't say I couldn't talk to certain family and they hadn't disowned me when I messed up, they were the perfect family in my eyes even though I knew no one was perfect.

I was also getting along well with New house friend, and I met the other girls. One of the girls liked bossing me around and wanted me to cook her food, so I did because last time I had stood up for myself I got kicked out. I had made a promise to myself to not make friends with people I lived with; it was the same rule I had made about school. I couldn't let friendship hold me back from getting schoolwork done, just like in my home life. There was too many arguments and fights. I then transitioned into the process of independent living and got to live in the unit. I was excited for my next step and I couldn't mess it up.

The first night there New house friend and I stayed up and decided to Facebook stalk all the workers. We were happy that we had found pretty much all the workers, but we weren't able to find one, who we didn't like anyway. She was the worst worker ever, she was worse than a worker that I had liked but Jade hadn't. We became closer friends, we hung out more, we skipped school and went to the mall for a girl's day, we got our nails done and had lunch. We didn't get into trouble because they didn't care that much. Being in the unit was fun and it was a great learning experience. We had $50 to spend and had to cook every night, except for weekends where we had dinner in the house. We also had lunch and breakfast in the house and spent all day in the house.

We had different types of worker, each one was cool in their own way. We had a worker who was more childish than some others, she loved Disney, flying kites and being childish, but she had a serious and caring side. We had an immature worker who was really cool but I didn't really like her. When I first arrived she bent the rules a bit, but was beyond caring, nice and she had a fun side. According to her she could be scary and she also understand us because she had gone through the same and probably worse. Then we had my favourite worker who was a Christian. She could be crazy and funny, but also really understanding. We had a worker who was artsy and I liked to bicker with her in a fun way and be sarcastic. We even had a worker who was like the mother of the house, if you told her she was wrong all hell would break lose. She was funny and everyone knew not to mess with her! Her favourite line was 'do you know who I am?' We also had another worker who was quiet, she is kept to herself and was a closed book. But she was funny and sometimes and bit blonde, but we loved her all the same. All of our workers were great people, except the one worker we don't like, and the other workers don't like her, so we just ignored her.

Even though I didn't want to make friends I was glad I had met someone like New house friend. She was like Jade in many ways; she did drugs but she was the next level of Jade. She had gone to jail and stole stuff, but like Jade I knew she needed someone to support her and influence her in a good way. I knew she was just struggling with herself and in life, so I hoped I might be the person she needed in her life to care about her and encourage her.

I had a youth night and I felt like God wanted me to ask her to come. The difference with my old home and new home was I was out of my comfort zone, here I was vulnerable which was a good thing because it meant I was open and ready for whatever God wanted to use me for. I was his vessel. I was sad that I wasn't this confident back home and I talked about God with the workers which was great. We had great chats but I also had a vision that I would see Jade as a Christian, but I never had the guts to ask her to a youth thing so I knew this would be my chance.

So I got up and asked her to come and to my surprise she said yes. I sent a message to my youth group and a couple of close friends, to Mama and Daddo, and asked them to all pray. We went to the youth event and it was amazing, such a great night and I had a smile on my face. This was where I belonged. I hadn't found a church I could call home because I guessed I wasn't ready to fully let go of my home church. But New house friend gave her life to Jesus and I was so proud of her. Becoming a Christian was such a big step but it was a big step towards a lifetime of happiness and love. I knew it was going to be hard and I prayed that God would give me strength and wisdom to be the best friend I could be and too support her in the way God wanted me to. I was scared, but I knew this was a new start, a new life, and I was ready for what God would bring no matter the struggles.

Every grandparent has their cooking specialty and I have found that Nans is chocolate balls. Like damn she makes incredible choc balls that puts anyones to shame. I loved my weekends away; they gave me a break and I went home refreshed.

My mental health was in check for a while and I didn't feel depressed, hadn't self-harmed in a couple of months which I was proud of. I did have a fall back a couple weeks before I moved into the unit, I was suicidal but I wasn't too bad. I did want to die but I didn't have a plan as such. We lived near a busy road, so I thought about jumping in front of a car. I was lucky that I still had my counsellor and my workers were really supportive. I had never had really caring workers before and I was able to open up to them. I was glad it had only lasted a couple of weeks. I think everything that had happened had come crashing down.

Now that I was in a better head place I could enjoy going up to the river with Ardy Pa and Nan, they were currently getting the block and creek ready for their new house boat that they would drive down to their block. I got to see the boat and even drive it! It was my first time on a houseboat and driving one is harder to steer then a normal boat, but still fun. When we were at the river I helped and it was good, I was getting used to sleeping there and hanging around the block. I went out on the tinnie to prune some branches off a tree to get the houseboat in and what an adventure that was.

Ardy acted like he loved living on the edge, a few times I was scared he was going to either fall into the water or cut his hand off. He even thought it would be good to say 'a ladder would be stable on here or maybe stilts.' I was not impressed and I said, 'I don't know first aid, you could hit your head, pass out, fall into the water and drown.' He thought I needed to lighten up because his excuse was 'it was adventures with Ardy pa.' I think we had different ideas on what an adventure was, his was more a suicide mission but I loved him nevertheless. Even if he came up with irrational thoughts and said things that probably shouldn't be said, I wouldn't want it any other way. They are wacky and crazy but so caring and loving, I am grateful for them.

I went to their church whenever I stayed over as well, and I enjoyed meeting new people. It made me feel loved and special whenever they introduced me as their granddaughter, they treated me more special than any other family had. Did I deserve it? No, I didn't, but I learned God gave us a lot, even if we don't deserve it because really, we don't deserve anything. I also had my own church that I went to with New house friend and that was good. The pastors were good friends with Mama and Daddo, so I had someone I knew.

I felt safe with Ardy Pa and Nan, I felt at home. I knew in my heart that I didn't have to search for another family, after years of searching aimlessly for a home and family to call my own and now I had found it. I was so scared to lose it I didn't want to let it go. I knew I had left home because of my mental health and childhood trauma because, let's face it, I couldn't control how I felt and how I let it out. I messed up and I was so afraid to mess up again. I message them asking if they would leave me and making them promise they would stay my parents. I wanted to trust them, but it was so hard. Tonight, was like any other night, I had dinner, a great day and I went to bed.

I was with Mama and Daddo and we were hanging out. Their faces were scrunched; they were angry and I was scared. What did I do? I tried being the best daughter I could be. 'We don't want you to be our daughter anymore, you hurt us and broke us, we are better off without you destroying our family.' Daddo said. The colour drained from my face as I looked at them and Baby B... no, no this can't be happing I scream.

I woke up in a cold sweat, 'it's okay it was just a dream,' I whispered trying to convince myself. Them not wanting me as a daughter, and them wanting to have their own family without me were my greatest fears. But I also knew that if that's what they wanted than I am going to have to deal with it and learn to cope. I didn't want to be fearful and I wanted to trust them when they said that they wouldn't leave. But how could I trust and love again when I'd been broken and rejected again and again?

It wasn't their fault, it was mine and I guess everything had affected me so much. Even if I had been affected by my past, I wasn't going to let the system break me. I'd seen it break people, friends and even family, but I knew I couldn't let it break me. I had to do it, for me and other kids in care. I knew it would take time until I could trust Mama and Daddo again. But I loved them just the same and was grateful for them and my grandparents, even if they were crazy.

I was enjoying the months and weeks of being happy, finally for the first time I felt free and happy, I felt like I belonged. I felt like this was home a feeling I hadn't felt since leaving home with Mama and Daddo, a feeling I never thought I could feel again. I got along with the workers yes, they annoyed me SO MUCH! But seriously, I was thankful for each one of them and I could trust them – we had great chats.

Sometimes I questioned them, especially when they said weird stuff about glow in the dark balls or religion or the flying spaghetti monster. Trust me its real, look it up! But as they said, I fitted in perfectly. And unfortunately, somethings go just as quickly as they come, sometimes even quicker. I knew this would come to an end and I was prepared. It was coming up to be a year since I had left home and I knew my mental health would dip I told my counsellor and a worker, just so everyone knew why I was going to be sad. It started with just an empty feeling and I cried a bit. Being the stupid person I am, I scrolled through messages and cried some more.

I hated how I had acted through the messages but I knew I was hurt. I was scared of letting go but I just didn't express it in a good way. But day after day I started slipping, I was getting worse, soon it was a week and I was becoming suicidal. I didn't want to live I had messed up so bad that I had hurt them. Yes they had forgiven me but I hadn't. I felt like I didn't deserve to forgive myself. I wanted to be with God in heaven, but I also felt that if I did go to hell I wouldn't be surprised, considering I messed up every family and placement ever.

One night I got bad and I needed to end my life, so I went to the servo down the road got a pack of Panadol and went to my room. That day nothing bad happened, I was stressed and angry, I swore and cried – I was overwhelmed. I went to my room, locked the doors and I heard my worker come in. I quickly hid the pills under my blanket, she came in and sat on my bed. She was close to the packet and I was scared she would find them. We talked and I felt bad that there was someone sitting right there showing they gave a damn, and I was going to end it all. Maybe I shouldn't do this, but I knew I had to, it was best for everyone. I cried and we talked, I was so sure that I had my mind-set on dying, I told her with my lip trembling 'this has to be done nothing will stop me.' She had always been a good worker, they all have, and I felt bad about what I was going to do – it wasn't their fault.

I was for sure closer to this worker then the others I think it was because she is a Christian too, so I got along better. Something that I didn't see coming was she looked like she was going to cry her eyes welling up, "what have I done" I thought to myself.

'I don't know if I am allowed to do this, but I don't care,' she said and then she asked me if she could pray for me. I nodded knowing that if I spoke my voice would break and I might break down. Her praying was the nicest thing someone could've done for me, and she didn't have to but I appreciated it. She gave me a hug and I could look at her, I was ashamed I hurt her and I couldn't look her in the eye. Instead I fiddled with my blanket holding back my tears. I knew I had to tell her that I had a pack of Panadol, I knew it wouldn't work I had been told many times to never OD on Panadol but it was split, irrational decision.

In the end, I told her and she got the pack and told me to come into the house. She had to ring an ambulance but I didn't want her to. I didn't have a choice though. I sat in another room and I didn't want to talk to anyone, but soon enough two ambo people came and I had to talk to them. I hopped into the ambulance, the drive to the hospital wasn't very long and I got to lay on the bed so that was good. Once at the hospital I had to get my vital checks and wait for the mental health team.

I chatted with New house friend while I waited for them, finally after a couple of hours I chatted with a dude. I opened up and told him everything that had happened and how I was feeling. But I didn't tell him why I was upset. He told me only I could keep myself safe and no one else could, which at the time I thought was absurd. If people didn't feel safe they reached out because when you were suicidal you couldn't stay safe. That's why you had a mental health team. I had never liked CAHMS, they have never helped in fact they'd made things worse. One day I hoped I could make the whole system better, because no kid deserved to go through what I had to go through. I had never heard a good thing about them and I was sure some helped but not the ones I had dealt with and my friends always had bad ones too.

I got sent home with them saying I was fine, and if I had to come back then I should come back. I was glad I had got to go home but I was annoyed that he didn't help. I hoped I never had to deal with him again. The only thing that was good that came from his mouth was getting new meds because mine sucked. On the way home, at like 3 am, driving back we saw a massive koala walk across the road. I was surprised because I see more koala's here in a big city than where I grew up in a small town-like city.

I didn't sleep in my room but on the couch in the house. It took me a while to fall asleep, but I got there eventually. A few nights later I was back in hospital and the same happened, so I went back home. This went on every couple of days, sometimes I lasted a week before going back. I didn't like all of this but the workers had a duty of care and it sucked. I ended up living in the house but I still got to do an independent shop. They wanted to make sure I was safer and where I could reach out. I didn't reach out when I was struggling until after I realised that what I was doing was dumb. Okay, suicide isn't dumb, but it wouldn't help. After I realised that I would make an effort to reach out. I did have a fear that one day it would get out of hand.

Being in the house was good, I got to go back into my Harry Potter room. It didn't stop me from hurting myself, as I had been told before, when you want to hurt yourself someone couldn't take everything away because in the end you would find something to hurt yourself with. It was a sucky thing but it couldn't be stopped until you found some other way to release the pain. I had never cut deep, just enough to bleed. It had stayed like that for a while and I brought so many pill packs but I would come back to be rational and realise that I couldn't do this. I knew deep down I didn't want to die I just didn't want to feel the pain I, wanted to forgive myself.

Then I started not going to school because I couldn't concentrate and school made it worse, so I would stay home. Georgia and I were on and off, so I didn't really have her and I couldn't talk the same with Lucy. But I had New house friend so that was good, and I was thankful for that. We also had a new girl arrive, I forced myself to be nice and make her feel welcomed even though I would have much rather avoided everyone.

I don't know where I would be without New house friend though, that girl had stuck up for me more than most people. She didn't take shit from anyone. One of the girls who liked bossing people around had called me many names, but New house friend would fight back. She was a good person who had just been misunderstood way too much. One night I said something along the lines of 'I get so bored during the day' and our smartass worker, who we have been complaining about for weeks, said 'maybe go to school.' I told her 'I had been in and out of hospital I was tired and not in a good headspace.' She replied with 'we all had our problems, deal with it like we all have to.' Now that pissed me off, when I was in a bad headspace it was like messing with a snake, I would fight back and would not stop.

What annoyed me was not just that she said that no, it was the fact that she had told us her problems and have said at times how she wanted, to kill herself something that us kids do not need to hear from a worker. So that night was not a good night for her because we swore at her and said no one liked her. I said things I shouldn't have said, and I swore like a pirate. I could've handled it better, but I don't have those skills so I exploded. In the end she shut the door on us, so New house friend nearly kicked in the door and we went for a stroll to a school nearby to hang out.

When we came back we were surprised that they hadn't placed an MPR (missing person's report) considering we were out after curfew. When we did come back the worker had all her stuff and said to us 'you girls will be happy that I'm leaving. She was meant to do a sleep over, and I replied 'good please don't ever come back,' and she left. We had KFC at 10:30 that night with two fill ins. I wasn't proud of my actions and no one deserved to be treated like that, but if I had the chance a part of me wouldn't say sorry. Though I know as a Christian I was called to say 'sorry and I forgive you' 70x7 times in fact. A week later she hadn't come back and we had a fill in, who at first I didn't like only because I don't like new people, but I started to like her. She was interesting and funny, especially when she couldn't get the car started.

I was planning on going back home to see my home church, Mama, Daddo and Baby B so I had to prove I was okay to go. I had to go because it was going to be our two-year family anniversary, so I needed to see them. I also hoped that there might be something about going away for a mini holiday that might cheer me up and make me feel better.

I was happy when I was told I could go to Lincol,n it was stressful planning, but I went and that was the main thing. I stayed for less than a week and the first couple of days I didn't do much. I walked around town, went into businesses that I knew and talked to people. Like last time when I went back for a visit I saw my old workers and I had good conversations. I missed them but I liked my workers now.

I hung with Jade for a bit and we walked around town. A week prior there was a smash in McDonalds, so the town was a bit anxious and stressed. They had a security guard in Target which I thought was a bit far. Yes a few years before some set fire to Target but no one actually liked Target because Kmart was way better. Jade and I had a great chat, we sat in McDonalds talking about how misunderstood kids were these days and how bad the system was.

I saw Lucy as well, it was all good until she talked about a guy she worked with who I didn't trust one bit, I was a protective friend but normal I warmed up to friends boyfriends until they broke my friends hearts, but this guy was different. I heard nothing but bad stuff about him so I was worried for her, but I knew if I said anything Lucy would get angry and snap so I didn't say anything just yet.

But then near the end of my stay she told me that they were dating, and I was stuck. Should I risk my friendship and say something that might not be true? Or should I say nothing and risk her getting hurt? Now I knew it was up to her to decide whether to believe me or not, I wasn't going to tell her never to be around him but I did message her saying, 'look I heard this I don't know if it was true and I hope it wasn't but I am going to tell you just in case.' Of course, just as I predicted, she got upset. I told her it might be wrong but she looked at it wrong.

He even messaged me saying that I was jealous, I laughed at that. I had a lot of guys messaging me, so I was not jealous, I was worried. But not everything went wrong because I saw other friends and I even got to spend time with Ash and her cute son. We went for a walk which was nice and talking to Ash made a lot of things better. Especially her amazing 'Ash' hugs that I loved, they were nearly as special as my Mama's hugs. I saw my counsellor which was also good because I don't see her much; we only talk on the phone. I was so excited to see Mama, Daddo and Baby B as I hadn't seen them since I had moved away; except I saw Mama when she came to Adelaide and we had a Mama-daughter date, something I have missed so much.

We just hung out and we had Grandma come over as well and we went out for lunch. I was very suss at the beginning because, you see, all year I had had a feeling they were going to be pregnant. Maybe it was just me loving being a big sissy or actually having amazing skills where I could predict the future. But every time we hung out they had to go to appointments and my predictions were wrong, but this day was different from the start. I had a gut feeling that it was going to be an amazing day. We had lunch and slyly I tried seeing if I could see a bump, but I couldn't. Well I didn't want to be caught but I was suspicious, I already knew they were going to an appointment after lunch.

We said goodbye and it was just Baby B, grandma and I. We went for a walk and this was another clue. During past appointments they took Baby B with them, could this just be a coincidence or maybe I might be right. I did enjoy my quality time with Baby B though, we went to the beach and the park and we played. I tried soaking up the quality time as much as I could before I would have to depart from them. And it broke my heart because when we first met up Baby B became shy, like she didn't know me but by the end, she ran up and hugged me.

We then started walking to the store because I gave Baby B some money. We met Mama and Daddo at the store from their 'car appointment' which could've fooled me considering they were getting a new car, but I couldn't be wrong this time. We went for a walk to the beach again and sat on the grass, and then what I have been waiting for happened. Daddo said 'we have some good news

Mama is...' did I let him finish? Ummm NO! I yelled so loud 'OMG YESSS!' I was so excited, even though I knew it was coming I was still so pumped I would get to be a big sissy.

Baby B had no idea and it was funny trying to get her to understand. We asked her 'do you want a baby brother or sister?' and her response was 'NO.' So we asked 'do you want to be a big sissy?' and she said 'yes.' I think what was more funny was Daddo saying 'mummy has a baby,' and turning to me saying 'I don't think I need to explain that you.' No one wants to know what their parents get up to, though I am lucky I have open parents. I said 'ew no please don't,' which made them laugh, and he replied '3 months ago Mama's feet were cold...' 'EW EW EW PLEASE STOP!' I said in disgust, blocking my ears and laughing. I didn't tell them that I had guessed, but I was still excited and couldn't wait to meet the little bean, I couldn't stop smiling.

I hadn't smiled this much for weeks, was this my turn around? I couldn't die and leave Baby B and little bean. We got into the car and I got dropped off, I was sad I couldn't spend more time with them but I was happy that I got amazing news.

After, at church I got to see my favourite people and what was my family when I had none. When sitting in church I felt so happy, I was home. The town wasn't home, this was home and then I realised I was going to miss this when I left. I was going to miss my pastors who have been so supportive and loving since a young age. I was going to miss my youth leaders and youth group and the band. But instead of thinking about what I was missing I smiled. I smiled because I was going to be a big sissy. I smiled for the future. I smiled for what God would use me for. I smiled for the kids I would one day help. I smiled for new beginnings, for a church I could come and visit, for new familys, and for a good God.

After church I packed and chilled until it was time to go to the airport. My worst nightmare was coming alive – it was not a clear sky! *It's okay it will clear up* I thought but after a while I got onto the plane, and to make it worse there was a bunch of people from my old school. I just had to hope I didn't get embarrassed. The flight, well the flight was what I feared. At the start it was good but then there were so many clouds and the turbulence was horrible. The engine sounded like it was stopping and starting, and the plane felt like it was dropping – like a horrible rollercoaster.

It was all grey out the window, I could feel the colour leave my face, I closed my eyes and tried to calm my bouncy knee and jittering hands. My anxiety was rising, and I was trying to pull it down. I wasn't going to die like this, I couldn't. I had so many things to do. Every bad thing I had done, all my sarcasm and being mean to my workers (even if it were a joke) I regretted it. I couldn't leave the world without righting my wrongs.

It was almost like my life flashed before my eyes and I decided there were two options: sit in my seat and have a panic attack while thinking about the good and bad stuff in my life; or read my bible. So that's what I did, with tears trying to fight their way out my eyes, I got my phone *God I can't die please just... just hold me, help me, calm down and don't let me die. I am sorry, I will do better just don't let me go. I have another baby sibling to care for and love and I will be better.* I cried silently, but luckily I was at the back of the plane which meant the people I knew couldn't see me make a fool of myself.

I opened my bible app, flicked to Psalms and read every bump and drop. I forced myself to focus on the words, not daring to let my eyes and mind wander. The more I read the more I felt calm, that was until another bump. I then decided that if I could make it to safety, I was going to tell all my workers I appreciated them because damn this was scary. I noticed there was a couple sleeping… SLEEPING! *How can they nap? Well I guess if I was asleep, I wouldn't know anything; and at the rate of my anxiety and quick breaths – if this goes any longer I would probably pass out because I felt so faint.*

After what felt like the longest 50 minutes of my life, we finally landed, and I got off the plane. My legs felt weak but I was so happy to not be on the plane. I am 100% certain I would not be going on a plane until the new year. Walking into the airport, I was just about to go and get my luggage, but I was still not completely over the plane ride. I was feeling numb and bit anxious when suddenly someone ran up and hugged me. I almost fell over and I had to take a couple of seconds to collect myself. 'Well I am glad someone missed me,' I said smiling at New house friend, with the worker trailing behind her. 'How was the flight?' she asked. 'I almost died!' I cried dramatically, but truthfully.

The drive home was pleasant, we talked about my time back home and we drove to KFC to get some tea. We talked a bit about a new girl that had just moved in and I was not excited to meet her. Apparently when she first came she said bad things about the house and hearing that hadn't make me too happy. But I also knew how being in a place that you don't know, and being new, can be scary and some people react differently. By the time we got home I was better. I was still numb and every now and then I would be shaky, but I was a lot better.

Once home I put my stuff in my room and talked with my other worker for a bit, we then decided to have go for a walk. I liked walking and chatting. While on the plane I had decided I was going to tell every worker that I appreciated them, some workers told me they will use it against me. Being nice and appreciative lasted about a week and then I was back to my normal sassy self.

But my happiness didn't last long either, soon I went back to being depressed and self-harming – all the stuff I was hoping wasn't going to happen after my trip away. I was getting worse; I was scared I couldn't fight to stay alive. I was losing the battle and I was so drained. I had little strength and I knew I should be leaning on God but I didn't, instead I put the last of my strength towards helping my two best friends were also struggling. I put them first, trying to help them, encourage them and support them. In my eyes they came first and just like when I lived in the group home/homeless shelter I spent my days helping others, and at night I would cry grab a blade and watch the blood, then wipe it up.

And the daily routine continued, sometimes (well most) days it ended up in either a police car or an ambulance to the hospital. I hated the hospital, I had to wait for hours, I lost sleep and I didn't get help. But sometimes I did tell my workers because I trusted them and a part of me did want help and to not die. But there was a part that wanted to die. So it was this war in my mind and heart, and it was tiring and draining. I didn't want to fight, my mind was so loud and busy. I had lost my mind and I don't even know what I am thinking half the time. I was lucky though because even though most workers at my old place were good people, every now and then I would think about them and I appreciate them, I wasn't supported as such. Whereas here the workers showed they actually gave a damn and wanted to help. They went out of their way to make sure I was okay. Through these hard times I did grow closer to some workers, we had a new worker who did the shift for the worker who no longer worked with us… whoops. I liked the new worker; she was fun to chat with and we went on one-on-ones. We drove with loud music and she also had horses, which I found out later on, and that was a big plus.

The ambulance and cops were also very nice and supportive, some made me smile and laugh. Sometimes my anxiety spiked, especially one night when I was trying to sleep I was having a bit of anxiety and then to make it worse I had some police come over and talk to me and I was shaking like crazy. The drive there was quiet, but after a while I felt okay and asked the police some questions. One of the nights my anxiety, again, was high and the hospital was worried, so I was hooked onto wires which wasn't as much fun. Every time I went to the hospital I had to have a worker with me and one worker was working in our house so it was good getting to know her, we played Uno and ate chocolate as it was nearly Halloween.

Another night I had another couple of officers come, the two guys were nice, and the chick was nice but you knew she meant business. After she had left it was just the two guys. One of them looked like Ed Sheeran, he had an orange beard but later on I found of he had no hair so now I call him 'Hairless Ed Sheeran.' The other guy was nice and funny too, they both would sarcastically bicker with each other which was fun to watch. 'You are way too nice to be a cop,' I said to Hairless Ed Sheeran. 'I can be mean,' he replied acting tough. 'Yeah sure.' I replied.

We were still waiting for the ambulance and then they decided to just take me. 'Could you please take me to McDonalds?' I asked eagerly but knowing they wouldn't. 'Yeah we can drive past them' they replied sarcastically and keeping to their word we drove past like three Maccas. 'Look there was McDonalds,' they said pointing at the fast food place. I rolled my eyes but decided to play their game, and when we were at the hospital I piped up 'oh look we are here, now let's go home,' but unfortunately, I had to go in. Even though I knew after a couple of hours they would send me home. I didn't want to stay in the mental ward but I knew I needed help and I wasn't getting it.

Before both of them had left Hairless Ed said he was working all week and he didn't want me to make him come up again. He was probably the best police officer I had met there after moving from home. He told me he actually cared and was worried, I told him I couldn't make any promises. While in hospital they planned for me to do a planned admission into the mental health ward, but I wasn't allowed to go to hospital until then. Unfortunately I couldn't just not be depressed and a part of me wanted help, so when I opened up to the workers I had to go to hospital. Once home I went to bed, I didn't go to church that day, I hadn't been for a while. One thing I had learned over the past three years of trial and pain was that no matter how bad I felt I needed to go to church, because it's what I needed to heal.

The next night, after having all my sharps taken away I bought some more, I went into the bathroom because I wasn't allowed in my room but then my worker wouldn't let me stay in the bathroom so instead she sat on the floor with me as I cried after a while I finally got up and left the bathroom and went into the kitchen I then left my phone home and decided to leave the house with one of the girls who I became friends with. It was past curfew and because we were at risk to ourselves the cops were called so we ran from them. Living in the hills meant we were running up and down the roads and we also went on the train. If I wasn't with her, I probably would go off somewhere alone and try to kill myself, but I couldn't leave her, she was struggling too.

I had lost all my strength, especially one night where I was on a soccer oval yelling at her in the rain and lightning, telling her that she needed to stay alive. That night I was so mentally, emotionally and physically drained and weak. I was on my floor crying my eyes out and I called out to God asking her to protect her because I couldn't. Tonight was the same and I stuck with her, I felt so sick from running and being anxious. We ran into many cop cars but they didn't see us, which was surprising.

They tried ringing her as my phone was still home and she didn't answer. Hairless Ed even tried getting me to answer, but she didn't want me to so I didn't. After a while we ran around the school next to home where the police tried getting up. Then we went to the skate park, I looked behind me and I saw a flashlight. I knew I didn't have anything in me to keep running so I stopped. I yelled out to her to stop too. It was the same guy from the night before, New house friend ran and out of nowhere like ten cars sped down the road like in the movies. We were both separated and searched. Once again my sharps were taken away and I was put in the car and taken back home. I got anxiety over EVERYTHING so in a fast police car I got anxious.

'Go to your room,' Hairless Ed said with a stern tone. *You're not my dad* I mentally said once I was in my room. We talked and I told him everything, the tears were burning so I let them out. 'I told you I can be mean' he said out of nowhere. 'No you aren't mean, you are just disappointed' I replied with a small smile. 'Yes, so don't do it again' he replied. I told him I was sorry and then I had to get my picture taken. Once the ambulance came I went in and sat on the chair, Hairless Ed asked if the cops had to come which he replied 'nah she is a good kid' while looking at me and nodding his head because I was staring at him blankly. Finally I copied him, he smiled and left.

Once at the hospital after a couple of hours I ended up being admitted into the mental ward. The bed was hard, harder than normal hospital beds and it took ages to fall asleep. I also didn't have my phone which meant I had no way to contact New house friend and I was worried about her. I needed to be there for her, she was now alone and she didn't really open up. I know she thought everyone would leave and I wanted to make sure she knew I wouldn't leave. The next I had to wake up early and sit around with a couple of the other kids and workers, we had to say what we were grateful for and all the boring stuff, then had breakfast. I kept to myself and didn't talk at all until I had a meeting with all these people, they wanted me to stay until Thursday which was a couple of days away as it was Tuesday. Even though I knew I needed the help I also knew I couldn't be away, I needed to make sure New house friend was okay. So finally, they let me go home. Once home my counsellor rang so I told her what had happen. She was going to ring on Thursday, but Wednesday I stayed up all night and ended up sleeping all day.

The night I ran from the police for many reasons; one of them was because I finally had workers who gave a damn but then I was told that they had all said I was doing it for attention, and that the police had said the same thing. It made me upset because I had major trust issues, so being told that was a set back and I didn't know if I should believe my friend or my workers. I did tell the workers and they reassured me a little, and after a while I just decided it wasn't worth the effort.

But against all odds, and though I feared I wasn't going to survive this, I learned that it wasn't a fight of the human body and mind but a spiritual battle. I learned this when I realised this was actually the worst I had ever been. I knew counsellors weren't going to help me, but God and the church could because of it being a spiritual attack. I needed to trust God and fight the devil, but I was too weak. After my time in hospital I gained my strength and fought it with everything I had. And what seemed impossible became possible: I was healed. I was getting better and only had God to thank. I started going back to church, met some more amazing people and just grew in strength mentally, emotionally and spiritually. Once I got better the other girls got better too, I was happy.

I kept going to both of my counsellors and tried getting better. I still had a lot to learn and so much past baggage I needed to work through. Some days I still messaged Mama and needed reassurance that they wouldn't leave because of being hurt so much. Not everything would be perfect, I still had issues where I lived and liked to take time for myself so I could recharge.

Week after week I noticed I had gotten better and others were noticing it to. My workers made sure that I knew that they were all so proud of me and how far I'd come, how much I have gotten better. This made me happy and made me want to keep fighting for the joy.

Some times when I saw Mama post on Instagram I would get a bit sad. One day, a week before Christmas, I was on YouTube I decided to google people I knew. After a few searches I got bored so I searched Mama's name and didn't see anything, so I did Daddo's and found a video of them talking to a church when they were in America a few months earlier. I started the video knowing full well

I was not going to be able cope watching. I started off strong but 16 minutes into the video the anxiety came bubbling up like a volcano. Feeling a panic attack coming on I left the house and went for a walk and started crying. Pulling out my phone I messaged Mama: 'why does it still hurt? It's been a year.' I don't know why it hurt so much but I knew I shouldn't have watched it.

I went home and cried on my bed eating chocolate. My worker came in and we talked; I didn't tell her what was wrong but she knew it was about the parents. We talked and laughed, shared embarrassing stories and cried. After, I got up and went to the bathroom to have a shower. While in there I had my laptop for music and dumbly decided to finish the video. Near the end they talked about me, it was good to know they still saw me as their daughter. They talked about how it hurt them and nearly broke them, which I already knew, but Mama said something that I wish I hadn't had to hear. She said how it made her feel with my bad mental health and past trauma it hurt so much to hear I dropped to the ground just like when I first moved out of home. I felt like my heart was ripped out of my chest, tears streaming out.

I messaged her really hurt, but that just led to a disagreement. She said that she felt like I wasn't letting her voice her hurt, so then I felt horrible. I spent a couple of days apologising even though I didn't think I should have to say sorry, but I was the kid so it is up to them. Mama and Daddo aren't bad people, they are the best parents I could ever ask for. But did it sometimes feel like I was always failing them? Yes. Did it feel like if I messed up, they would leave? 100%. But I didn't want to live life without parents and I trusted them that they wouldn't leave, and that it wouldn't always feel like this. I wanted to look towards the future.

A thought did come to my mind *Why am going through the hurt? What if it doesn't work, then I'm going through this hurt and nightmare for nothing*, but I knew it wasn't the case. I refused to think about the hurt and let that decide if I should stay their family. I wanted to wait for it to get better rather than to give up because of temporary pain, hurt and dreams.

I was seeing Mama, Daddo and Baby B for Christmas eve and I was excited, but I was a bit scared it would be awkward because of our disagreement. Christmas eve came though and I quickly realised there was nothing to fear. We had a great brunch and Baby B loved her presents. Ardy Pa and Nan came as well because I was staying with them for a week. I was so excited to have time away for a break and recharge before the new year, where I would be working towards living alone and finding a job.

After our brunch it was time to say bye, I didn't expect it to be hard but little Baby B looked up at me and said 'sissy come back with me,' in her little 2 ½ year old voice. 'I'm sorry baby but you have to go with mummy and daddy,' I replied my heart was hurting for her. 'No I want to stay with you.' She had gone through the year learning that I didn't live at home anymore but I guess she was getting big. I don't know, but when we walked to the car she said 'you stay here, and I will pick you up from the airport.' It hurt knowing she missed her big sissy but it showed how much she loved and looks up to me, I guess.

I was glad I didn't have to spend Christmas alone this year. There was a void in my heart because I wished I was home and wasn't just 'visiting Mama and Daddo'. But it was what it was, and I knew I didn't have a choice but to focus on the good. Yes it had broken me but was it breaking me or teaching me to be resilient and strong? I guess I wouldn't know until I came out of this. The workers at the placement were very nice and got us girls presents. The time in this house had made me come out of my comfort zone, trust, learn new things and grow to become a better person.

They were like family; always there to support me, make me laugh, help me grow and annoy the hell out of me; but looking at each kid and worker they were all special and would always be in my heart. Just like being with Mama, Daddo and the grandparents they made me cry but the love I had for them would never cease. I smiled thinking about how lucky I was no matter how much it hurt, how much I cried or wishd it was different. I now had people to fall back on (I hoped).

The week away was what I had needed, I grew closer to God and hungered to grow closer. But it all changed when I went home becase after a while I began self-harming again. But this time it wasn't from depression, but my anxiety, which was playing up. I didn't feel safe at home and wished things were better. I knew I had to fight for joy, and I didn't want anyone feeling how I felt. I didn't care if people didn't like me, I would stay in my room a lot because I liked having my own space; but my worker and I made a deal that she wouldn't smoke if I didn't cut.

I didn't know where life would take me but I know I would have good days and bad days. At times I wanted to die but I knew every time God would save me. And if I could help people then life was worth living. The system had tried breaking me; sin had tried breaking me – but nothing could hold me down. I would fight for joy, for my baby siblings, my nieces, and the kids in care who were alone.

On my knees, arms raised in the air, I would yell 'God I choose you. I will always choose you.'

And with God by myside, my family behind me and my future in front I would walk forward and never turn back.

EPILOGUE

If someone is passionate about something that needs to improve or change they can't just protest without having a plan about how to improve or change that thing. The foster care system needs to change so much. No kid should ever have to move from home to home. It makes me sad seeing kids from a young age in a group home. I also had social worker after social worker. I knew people whose social workers had changed so much in short span of time. Not that it's their thought. So how can it improve?

From experience I have been passed through families that weren't equipped and needed more training. Unfortunately, love can't fix everything; not earthly love anyway. It does help, but new carers need to know how to support a kid who has experienced so much trauma and past hurt. We have built a wall around our hearts and we push and push because that's all we have ever known.

Mama and Daddo were and are the best parents I could ask for and I am forever grateful, but they had a kid with mental health issues so they didn't know what to do to help me and they didn't receive support either. It's a two-way street. Unsupported new foster carers can't support years of trauma. And though it hurt to leave I knew I couldn't blame them. There were days I wanted to hate them, but I couldn't.

And social workers aren't to blame because they are pressured with so many kids to look after. There is a small number of workers and a whole lot of kids. I learned that I couldn't blame the social workers when they were trying to help.

I have heard so many people say that teens in care aren't good people: 'they are traumatised, get into crime and drugs.' We are labelled as 'troubled'. Yes, some of this may be true, but we are kids and we need to be loved. We need to know people aren't going to leave; that we are worthy of love and care. People want little kids because 'they are easier,' well that's what they think. But even those kids would grow up and turn into teens; and I know that when I saw how people wanted little kids it made me feel like I was not as worthy.

So many people I know push others away when they show care. I am guilty of this; but what makes me sadder is when I hear my friends and people my age say things like 'you will leave, everyone does,' and 'you will stop caring soon.' I used to say stuff like this and sometimes I still do, or I wonder why no one wanted me. Why my own biological family didn't want me. *What have I done so wrong?*

I know now that it wasn't our fault, we have been let down by people who shouldn't have let us down. We can't blame ourselves; we are the kids and they are the adults. Giving new foster parents support and more training may not completely fix the problems, but it would help. Giving social workers support and getting more of them to work allows them more time to spend with and help the kids that they have to help. To make sure that the kid's new family is the right fit.

Us foster kids, we are thrown to the side and misunderstood; told to act like adults but are treated like kids. We are told we couldn't say what we thought and felt because we didn't know what we were talking about. We are overlooked. We deserve a voice, to be treated like other kids and to be heard – able to make the decisions that impact our lives.

I don't know what the future will bring, I don't know if Mama and Daddo will stay my parents or if my chosen family will stick around, or if I will be able to make an impact. But I do know that God is good. I can start a chain reaction, get into Uni and become a better person. I also know we are not broken, we are just in a broken system. It's hard rising above the system and the stereotypes, but we have to find the crack where the light is shining in. To keep swimming and prove everyone wrong. We are better than this, we aren't just 'foster kids'; we are strong, powerful, beautiful and amazing people.

We weren't prepared for half the stuff we went through, but we did and always will get through it, because the demons don't deserve to win.

ACKNOWLEDGMENTS

Before I say anything else, I would like to say Thank you to God because without him this book wouldn't be possible. Without him I wouldn't call myself the author of this book because God should be the author. God, Thank you for being there for me, for sending your son to die on that cross, for me you sent him to die knowing to well that some of us wouldn't love you back, thanks for answering my prayers and holding me through the storms. Thanks for being such a good father, for putting people in my life who have helped me to grow.

It took a lot of time, effort, questions and love to write this book. Like most books I poured my heart into it in the hope I could help someone who may be going through something similar, or just going through a rough patch in life. I wrote this book to show that no matter what you may be going through you are strong and you can get through it because you have more strength then you know. 'You are way too strong to give up.'

Thanks to the publishers and editors at Green Hill, without you my book wouldn't be this amazing. Without you guys I wouldn't be able to show people how strong they are and how they can get through anything. I wouldn't be able to tell my story, so thank you! Thanks for not giving up on me or my book. You all have been a blessing and I hope to work with you guys again. Thank you also to Haydn Kuchel for your support during the crowdfunding campaign.

Thanks to all my carers; Lisa and Grant, Jane, Mama and Daddo, and all the others that I have lived with. Thanks for the never ending support, there were hard times and some of us didn't get along and the placement didn't last long but I guess it wasn't meant to be at the time. In the end we became closer than before so thank you for continuing a relationship with me after my departure from each placement.

Mama and Daddo, I would like to especially thank you for loving me like no other, for loving me even when I wasn't loveable, and for using your time and effort to support me and help me grow. For teaching me how to love and trust again, for being my heart adopted parents even after I left. I seriously can't say thanks enough. I love you both so much, thanks for the messages and for continuing to be my parents and always reassuring me that you will still be my parents. I will always love you and see you as my parents and I can't wait to see where God leads us as a family.

I would also love to say thank you to Baby B for being the best baby sister, for loving me when I failed you, and for never forgetting me. You changed my life princess!

Thank you to the placements, like the group home, Sonia and Brenton, Michelle who gave me a roof over my head until I found a home. I couldn't thank you guys enough.

Tim and Jess: thanks for believing in me when I didn't believe in myself, for loving me and showing and teaching me to keep my head up. Thanks for never leaving my side, I love you guys! Thank you for filling in as my parents when I left placement, you guys are amazing. Without your support I worry what I could've turned too and I'm glad that I have you and glad you helped me go in the right direction. Thanks for the prayers and just being there for me to talk to.

My youth group: thanks for being supportive and never leaving my side, for picking me up when I fell, for being so encouraging and just incredible God fearing and loving people. Life wouldn't have been as enjoyable without you guys and you are seriously my family. Especially, Shekinah, Sabrina and Taylah.

Ana and Ben: thanks for all the support, advice and love. Thank you Ben for teaching me guitar and encouraging me even when I felt like I failed! You two are incredibly important to me. Ana, no words will ever describe how much you mean to me and how important you are to me. Thank you so much for all the times you were there for me and for putting your problems aside for me. Thanks for always being one text away, for the chats and hugs. You are such an incredible person and I thank God every day for you.

Thanks to the extended family, like gran, grandma, Kayla, Ardy pa and nan, Nicole and Benji. You guys brought me in and treated me like family when I didn't have anyone. You guys loved me for who I was and saw me as your cousin/niece/granddaughter/god-daughter even though I wasn't your blood family. You taught me the power and love of heart adoption which is something that I hope I can keep in the family, and maybe one day heart adopt a kid too.

Thanks to my pastors who helped me grow and love God. Even more for supporting me.

Thanks to my church at home and here in Adelaide for praying for me, even if some of you didn't know me that well.

Thanks to Georgia and Lucy for sticking by my side through thick and thin, for loving me and supporting me, for the prayers and advice. We didn't always get along, but we always said sorry and I forgive you.

Geo, I couldn't thank you enough. You are such an incredible person, where I would be without you? I don't know. I love you so much. You are my best friend and sister that I got to choose. I couldn't ask for better friend, I know we will be friends for a long time! So, thank you. I don't know where I would be without you, I have enjoyed watching you grow in your faith.

Thanks to the place I live in now, all you workers are incredible, funny, weird and the best support. Thanks for dealing with me and being you! Thanks for the chats, drives and laughs. My best memories last year and this year have been while living here.

Thanks to other special people in my life and my family. Thank you Ash for being a special person who never gives up on me, you will always mean so much to me. Thanks to all the funny and cool people I met here in Adelaide. And obviously, thanks to my girls Jade and Cheryl. I don't know where I would be without you two, love ya. And to my big sister, thanks for being the only biological family that I am close to and for the best baby niece.

To my other nieces, know I love you so much and miss you. Eldest sister, I love you.

And lastly thanks to YOU, thanks to all my readers for reading my book. I hope you enjoyed it and it has helped you and has reminded you that you are strong. You can get through it no matter how hard life is – you guys are awesome.

www.ingramcontent.com/pod-product-compliance
Lightning Source LLC
LaVergne TN
LVHW040150080526
838202LV00042B/3103